Essential Mentoring Skills

Essential Mentoring Skills

A practical handbook for
school-based teacher educators

PAUL STEPHENS

STANLEY THORNES (PUBLISHERS) LTD

First published in 1996 by:
Stanley Thornes (Publishers) Ltd
Ellenborough House
Wellington Street
Cheltenham
Glos. GL50 1YW
UK

A catalogue record for this book is available from the British Library.

ISBN 0 7487 2247 5

Typeset by
Northern Phototypesetting Co Ltd, Bolton
Printed and bound in Great Britain by
Redwood Books Limited, Trowbridge, Wiltshire

Contents

Acknowledgements

Writing this book proved a challenging venture. It made me think deeply about my own practice as a teacher and a mentor. It also forced me to make that practice as explicit as possible. But this wasn't enough. I needed the advice and guidance of other people: teachers, mentors, university tutors, and I received it generously. Without their expert counsel, the book would have been based on just my experience and my opinion.

First and foremost, the inspiration to write this book came from two people who were 'mentors' to me: the late Steve Schenk, who taught me sociology and supervised my Ph.D. in that subject at the University of London; and Denis Devine, who supervised my teaching practice when I was a PGCE student at Digby Stuart College, London. Their brilliance as teachers and their wise counsel have had lasting effects on my own beliefs and practices.

I'm especially indebted to Dr Bob Campbell, Dr Ian Davies, Dr Chris Kyriacou and Professor Ian Lister, University of York, for their expert guidance and unstinting support in all my mentoring work. The insights I received from these mentors: Dr Steve Beer, Howard Campion, John Carr, Brian Cowie, Tim Crawley, Ann Ferguson, Ian Henderson, Gary Martin and Indru Nariani were inestimable.

Tim Crawley and Denis Devine deserve special thanks for reading and correcting the completed manuscript, and for making important contributions to the final version through their criticism and suggestions.

A big 'thank you' goes to Rhian Saia, an art teacher in my school, for doing the excellent illustrations in this book. My gratitude extends to Beryl Black, the school's professional tutor, for all her encouragement during the writing of *Essential Mentoring Skills*, and to Paul Hirst, the school's curriculum manager, for his very helpful and generously given advice on assessment.

My publisher, Francis Dodds, was kind, patient, encouraging and exacting, all rolled into one; for these qualities, I owe him much.

Finally, I must thank these important people: Laurence Job, Victoria Manley, Amanda Murphy, Kevin Rogers and Carla Stobie, whom I mentored recently during their PGCE secondary course, and whose comments on how mentors can best help student teachers proved invaluable; my school students for always (well, nearly always!) being kind to me; and Dr Peter Tomlinson, University of Leeds, for sharing his very astute and convincing thoughts on effective mentoring with me.

Paul Stephens
York, November 1995

Note

In July 1995 the Department for Education (DfE) merged with the Employment Department to become the Department for Education and Employment (DfEE). Throughout this book reference is made to the DfEE where current policy is concerned, even though that policy was published by the DfE. References to the Bibliography (e.g. DfE, 1993) make clear the actual source of policy directives cited.

Dedication

For Mum, Dad, Philip, Patty, Jessica and Benedict. Thank you for always being there.

CHAPTER 1

Becoming an effective mentor

When people ask me what job I do, I don't usually tell them I'm a mentor. 'I'm a teacher' creates far less confusion. Tell someone you're a mentor and, unless they're one too, they'll think either that you're just off the set of a new Dr Who series, or that you're the guide and adviser of the young Telemachus – a character in Homer's *Odyssey* – whose name was Mentor.

The second assumption is actually closer to the truth, because modern-day mentors, like their ancient Greek predecessor, are supposed to be experienced and trusted guides and advisers. Unlike our prototype, however, we mentors of the 1990s are the school-based educators of future teachers. Our brief has been given added momentum in recent years by the decision of the then Department for Education (DfE) to make initial teacher education more 'closely linked to its practical application' (DfE, 1993a).

In that context, 'schools should not only act as full partners with higher edu-

1

cation institutions, but should also be able, if they wish, to play the leading role in planning and providing courses' (DfE, 1993a). In either of these two options, the partnership or the autonomous model, mentors have a crucial role to play. For they are where the action is: in the schools. It's there that mentors have gained the professional expertise which they now seek, within the daily practice of their craft, to make available to the teachers of tomorrow.

This book is written by a mentor for mentors and other experienced teachers who want to make the art of teaching accessible for others. While it gives some background consideration to the most recent reforms in initial teacher education, it is, above all, a 'hands on, can do' handbook. The emphasis is very much on tried and tested practical mentoring strategies that can be realistically adopted by busy teachers who know the meaning of 'administrative overload'. Being a teacher and a mentor myself, I know and understand the world in which you work.

The book may also be of interest to the campus counterparts of mentors: university tutors of education. For the most part, and properly so, the tutor works in partnership with the mentor. It helps therefore, in order to forge a productive relationship, that each partner knows what the other one is doing.

Other interested readers might be deputy and headteachers and professional tutors in schools, all of whom play an important role in the initial teacher education of student teachers. Office for Standards in Education (OFSTED) inspectors, who are the 'quality controllers' of initial teacher education courses, are also likely to find the book helpful and informative. So too might Department for Education and Employment (DfEE) and local education authority officials, all of whom, in their different ways, are required to take into account the latest reforms in school-focused teacher education.

This book is concerned with reflective practice. Effective mentors are dispensers of know-how, but they're contemplative too. I think that good mentoring becomes even better when its exponents are also principled practitioners, and when they promote principled practice among those who would be teachers.

By 'principled' I mean – and this is expanded upon in Chapter 3 – striving to make teaching an emancipatory profession: one that liberates the learning potential of school students, while at the same time treating them with dignity and respect.

More specifically, becoming (or being) an effective mentor – in my opinion – means helping student teachers to make progress on the following important fronts:

- acquiring and developing beginning competence in and commitment to these goals: attaining appropriate and secure subject knowledge; making that knowledge accessible and interesting to school students; accurately, compassionately and diagnostically assessing their learning; good-naturedly managing their behaviour and learning; caring for and promoting their psychological, social and material welfare; being able to handle basic computer applications; and dealing with routine (at least to begin with!) administration

- possessing and applying a critical understanding of differing learning, teaching, class management and pastoral theories and practices
- finding ways to practise and promote social justice in their professional work, and thereby acknowledging that being a teacher requires ethical and 'political' commitment.

The main focus of the book is on secondary school mentoring. However, primary school mentors will also benefit by reading *Essential Mentoring Skills* because good mentoring is founded on generic skills and qualities that apply to teacher educators working with school students of all ages.

This introductory chapter outlines the basic features of mentoring work in secondary schools. It does this with reference to my own experiences as both a subject and, more recently, a whole-school issues mentor in a large, urban comprehensive school on the outskirts of Leeds. I draw too upon my work with co-teacher educators at the University of York (with whom my school and some fifty other secondary schools co-work as members of the York Partnership). The shared thoughts and practices of nine mentors who work in the North of England are also featured in the book. So too are the findings of important recent research into school-based teacher education, some conducted by myself, some reported in very up-to-date publications. The most recent books on mentoring that I found especially helpful are listed in the Bibliography with a brief descriptive comment.

The DfEE's current policies on school-based teacher education are briefly introduced in this chapter, and are described more fully in Chapter 2. These policies underpin not just an extended 'teaching practice', but a radical shift in the design and organisation of the education of tomorrow's teachers. As part of that process, mentoring is becoming an important means of professional development for those outstanding classroom teachers who still want to remain frontline practitioners. Chapter 3 (an adaptation of a chapter (Stephens, 1995) I wrote in *Schools in Partnership*) takes up the issue of principled practice, showing mentors how to foster conscientious teaching, as well as being skills instructors. Chapter 4 outlines and suggests ways of effectively implementing key generic professional skills that all mentors need to acquire and develop.

More targeted guidance on how mentors can most successfully provide helpful observation, relevant classroom practice, insightful debriefings, and realistic, supportive assessment for intending teachers in the DfEE-designated competences expected of newly qualified entrants to the profession, is given in Chapters 5–7. The very classroom-specific skills of subject knowledge and application, and class management are examined in Chapter 5. Assessment of school students' progress is considered in Chapter 6, and the wider realm of whole-school issues (rather curiously referred to as 'professional development' by the then DfE), is discussed in Chapter 7.

Throughout the book, I've assumed that the majority of mentors will be working in partnership with university tutors of education. That's the typical model as things stand at the moment, and I anticipate no significant change in the future. Professional work requires a higher education base, as well as 'on the job training'. Nevertheless, *Essential Mentoring Skills* may also be of use to those few mentors who are the sole providers of initial teacher education, either through one school, or, more usually, in a consortium of several schools. After all, school-based teacher education, whether in partnership with higher education or on its own, is always going to be a 'chalk-on-the-hands' experience.

It's now apposite then to consider what practical mentoring work entails in a modern comprehensive school.

Getting to grips with mentoring: the preliminaries

Let's hope you're not in a school where, on the last day before the summer recess, your headteacher informs you that you're going to be a mentor when you return in the next school year. Such things happen, but this kind of situation hardly gives you much time to get ready for your new job. It probably suggests too that you work in a school where the senior management are not taking the important task of school-based teacher education as seriously as they ought to. Mentoring only flourishes when it's perceived by senior managers as an important aspect of staff development rather than a tiresome burden to be landed on unwilling and unprepared shoulders.

Don't feel that you're not up to the task, though. The fact that you've been selected as a mentor means your headteacher knows you're an effective teacher. By reading this book and acting on the professionally grounded experience it offers, you'll become an effective or a more effective mentor. That applies whether you've been inducted into the basics of mentoring before you take on the job for real, or, less sensibly, rushed into your new role. Even experienced mentors will find the book offers insights, advice and guidance that will help them to improve the work they're already doing.

So let me start by telling you something about my mentoring background and what I've learnt in my professional capacities as, initially, a subject mentor, and, more recently, also as a whole-school issues mentor.

Subject mentoring

Although I had two years' experience as a secondary school teaching practice supervisor behind me, my work as an officially designated subject mentor began in September 1993. As head of social sciences in a large comprehensive school in the north of England, I was now to be a full partner with my teacher educator colleagues at York University in the initial teacher education of five intending teachers. For that's the difference between being a teaching practice supervisor and a mentor: supervisors follow the instructions of campus education tutors; mentors set the agenda with the tutors.

I wasn't kick-started into this new responsibility, but had indicated, during my statutory teacher appraisal, that this was an area I wanted to move into. My professional tutor – that is, the colleague who takes overall responsibility for school-based initial teacher education – responded favourably to this overture. She informed me, some six months prior to the commencement of my forthcoming post, that I would be a subject mentor to five graduate social science student teachers for the 1993–4 school year.

Elation, coupled with panic, were the first reactions. But, before beginning my new job as an officially designated subject mentor, my professional tutor invited me to lead a school-based day on 'equal opportunities across the curriculum' for 20 student teachers. She briefed me thoroughly on what this entailed, and let me enlist her expertise and services and those of other experienced teachers on the day. In effect, she created a useful dress rehearsal for the kind of work I would be doing some six months on. And that day went very well indeed: I was ready for it, having done plenty of prior conferring and preparation.

So here comes my first piece of advice. Whenever possible, cut your teeth on a practice go at mentoring before you take up your official duties. It's not necessary to lead an entire event: great if you can, but shadowing and assisting an existing mentor for a day or so is also helpful. Next, arrange an informal briefing with your co-teacher educators at the partnership university or, in the case of school-led ventures, at the schools in the consortium. Certainly, it would be reasonable to expect and to ask your headteacher for a day off-site in order to do this. At this meeting, it's vital that you obtain as much information as possible about the initial teacher education course that you'll be working on: not just your specific mentoring role but an overview of the whole operation. That way, you'll be able to ensure that what you do is in accord with the work of your co-teacher educators, both school and campus-based. When, for example, my student teachers study communication skills on campus, I support this out-of-classroom exercise with a practical follow-up in school on the same issue.

Once you've had some 'dry-run' mentoring practice and have been fully briefed on how your role slots into the wider picture, it's time to start preparing your own personal schedule.

Preparation for student teacher placements

Firstly, you'll need to negotiate with your senior colleagues a suitable amount of non-contact time to conduct individual or group tutorials with your student teacher(s). In my experience, 70 minutes (a double period in my school) weekly is the absolute minimum amount of time needed to do a reasonable job here. More, of course, would be better. Quote me on that if this reasonable expectation is met with incredulity on the part of colleagues who are responsible for staff timetabling.

Secondly, it's necessary to provide student teachers with their individual timetables. In the York Partnership, student teachers spend two days weekly at one school and three days weekly on campus during the first and last terms of the one-year course. In between these two periods (that is, during the second term), they spend five days weekly at a different school on a three months' 'main placement' – the current equivalent of the old-style 'main block teaching practice'. They therefore require three timetables: the first and third ones provided by the school where I work, and the second one provided by the school where the main placement is conducted. Given though that there are also student teachers who do their initial and final school placements at schools other than mine, mentors at my school are additionally responsible for providing these interns with a main placement timetable when they're with us.

Allowing for some differences between your scheme and mine, here are the main steps that need to be taken in getting ready for the arrival of full-time, one-year course, student teachers on school placements:

1 Find out, through prior communication with the tutor and the student teachers, what the student teachers are qualified for and want to teach. It's also helpful to enquire about any additional experiences they'd like to acquire during the school placement. For example, some of them might express a willingness to become involved in extra-curricular activities, like after-school computer clubs and weekend orienteering courses. Whenever possible, do your best to see that any such extras feature in or are appended to the student teacher's timetable. As an important partner in the professional development of intending teachers, it's your responsibility to ensure that the programme they encounter is as rich and as varied as possible.

2 On the basis of the information obtained from the above consultation, construct a prospective timetable and send copies of it to the university tutor and the student teachers. The assembling of this consultative document will involve conferring with other teachers whose expertise will feature prominently in the mentoring programme you organise. For example, in a main

placement timetable for a student teacher whose first subject is English with PE as a subsidiary, you might have the student working with your classes for three days, and with the classes of another English teacher and a PE teacher shared between the remaining two days of a normal school week. While, of course, first-subject teaching is a priority, do leave room (perhaps a couple of hours weekly) for second-subject teaching, even if this is only on a co-teaching basis.

3 Once you've received feedback from the tutor and the student teachers, arrange induction visits for the student teachers (two days would be good) prior to the actual placement in order to make any necessary adjustments to the timetable. In drawing up the final schedule, be prepared to make further modifications during the placement if circumstances warrant this. It's important to ensure that student teachers obtain the right balance of observation, collaborative and solo teaching, shadowing of departmental meetings and parents' evenings, and other experiences relevant to the wide-ranging curriculum responsibilities of the subject specialist. Don't let such matters take care of themselves; they require detailed advance planning and plenty of consultation with subject teacher colleagues and co-teacher educators.

A balanced timetable

As a general principle, the observation of experienced teachers (not just with you; variety is important and it reduces the risk of the 'copy-cat syndrome') and some co-teaching with both student and qualified practitioners, should figure prominently in the first couple of months of the school-based programme. In most cases during this period, student teachers will be on campus for two or three days weekly. Within a month or so, the majority of them will be ready to go solo in small doses under the supervision of the mentor. Perhaps they might introduce a new topic, using appropriate resources (OHPs, computers, VCRs, etc.) for the first 20 minutes, before moving into a co-teaching, but still a lead, role with you. It's important that this first solo cameo has been properly rehearsed beforehand: yourself and some other student teachers would make a good audience. Make sure too that the class is well chosen to maximise the prospect of a positive first encounter. It's also crucial, from a health and safety standpoint, that your student teacher knows you're always close at hand and on call should circumstances warrant your intervention.

Your timetables should be sufficiently flexible to allow for different rates of progress, but consider introducing student teachers to a fair amount of solo teaching during their second term at school – which, for many of them, will be their main placement. At least a third of this should be unobserved. Student teachers need to find their own feet, and they won't be able to do this if the mentor is over-protective or keeps an eye on things all the time. Half a qualified teacher's timetable is about right for solo teaching, with the remaining half divided equally between co-teaching and non-contact activities.

The non-contact time should include:

- pre-lesson discussions and planning with mentors and other teachers
- post-lesson debriefings when mentors and other teachers have been observers or when they've been observed by student teachers
- the continuing observation of qualified teachers, with opportunities to experience a range of different skills and styles
- the shadowing of mentors and other teachers when they go about their non-contact curriculum duties, for example at departmental and parent meetings, and during the marking of assignments and tests.

This second-term placement should form the substantive part of subject mentoring. Thereafter, and for the remainder of the school-based part of the course (which usually involves a couple of days or so on campus in many partnerships), it's helpful to provide the student with as much time as possible for reflective practice. That isn't to suggest that a fair amount of reflection hasn't already occurred. However, in the final stage of initial teacher education, student teachers will have more experiences to reflect upon than previously.

In the York Partnership, the last three months of the programme return to the three days on campus/two days at school model (the school being the original first placement school). I timetable the amount of teaching (solo and collaborative) student teachers do to about two half-days, and I devote the remaining two half-days at school to their discussing educational ideas and strategies with myself and as many teachers as possible. This should involve teachers in a variety of subject areas and teachers who display different class-management styles. These teachers will have to surrender some of their non-contact time for this purpose. I find that colleagues are exceptionally generous about such matters. Moreover, they also gain some useful mentoring experience. Offer student teachers some practice job interviews (with you as the interviewer) too. It's something they really appreciate.

As always, what happens on campus shouldn't remain in 'splendid isolation': link it to the school experience. If student teachers and university tutors are discussing IT use in Key Stage 3 history, for example, when they come to school, get them working alongside some Key Stage 3 history students who are accessing historical data from a CD-ROM.

Introducing student teachers to the school

During the induction days, once their timetables have been arranged, it's an excellent idea to provide student teachers with some background information about the school and the department(s) where they'll be placed. I prepare a concise written 'Guide for student teachers' on the ethos and goals of my school and my department, which I send to the students even before they start their placement. We then discuss these matters further when they're on the school premises.

Also during the induction days, I give student teachers a plan of the school, and I get school students to give them a whole-school tour, as well as a school student's perspective on the institution. I introduce student teachers to the colleagues they'll be working with, and I acquaint them with the 'etiquette' of staffroom culture. I give student teachers a tour of the departmental area where they'll be based, and I make sure they know what resources are at their disposal, and, as appropriate, how to book equipment and specially equipped rooms (e.g. audio-visual and IT suites). I ensure too that student teachers are briefed on: the length and structure of the school day; procedures for reporting their absence; where they can work during non-contact time; and how they can get a school dinner. Finally, I inform them about: important health and safety regulations (including how to differentiate a fire alarm from a recess bell, and how to evacuate the building); the school 'dress code' (staff, as well as school students); and the generally accepted norms and procedures governing relations between school students, student teachers and teachers.

Now it's time to say something about the education of student teachers in areas of the school experience that extend beyond subject teaching.

Whole-school issues mentoring

The whole-school issues mentor takes responsibility for guiding and instructing student teachers in the administrative, health and safety, and pastoral aspects of education: how to keep a good register; how to handle suspected child abuse; how to deal with the fears and tears of a bullied child.

These are generic issues that affect all teachers, whatever their subject specialism. In that respect, they rightly remind us that we're not merely teachers of knowledge and skills, but also members of a caring profession. While a compassionate attitude should feature in all aspects of subject teaching, there are also times in a teacher's work that need to be set aside for those parts of school student development and growth that the school curriculum doesn't reach!

Timetabling arrangements for whole-school issues might usefully be arranged on a one-day-a-week basis when student teachers are also attending campus sessions. In the York Partnership, all student teachers, whatever their subject specialism, are provided with a common once-weekly whole-school issues programme during their first and last placement. On this particular day, the kinds of question that student teachers have already considered on campus are supported and extended in a practical context. In the scheme to which my school is attached, an additional day at school is devoted to subject-specific issues. The scheme works like this:

The first term of initial teacher education contains:

- a once-weekly whole-school issues day at university which considers a particular theme, for example, equal opportunities
- a once-weekly whole-school issues day at school that focuses on the same question in a practice context, and that occurs on the day after the campus session
- twice-weekly specialist subject days at university that examine curriculum and pedagogical issues
- a once-weekly specialist subject day at school that, whenever possible, links, 'chalkface-wise', with the two campus sessions.

The second term of the course is entirely school-based, and it's up to mentors to organise a timetable that contains both subject-specific and whole-school issues experiences. The third term reverts to the first term pattern, with special emphasis on reflective practice (and on getting a job!).

Whatever variant on the above model you work with, it's best to begin with 'theory' and follow up with 'practice'. For example, as part of a whole-school issues programme, a campus discussion on class-management styles might usefully be accompanied by collaborative work with teachers who manage classes in different ways. Post-practice discussion with these teachers will help student teachers to make sense of what's happened in the classroom. This last discussion phase is very important; make sure you build it into the whole-school issues timetable.

Programme components

It's now appropriate to say something about the kind of matters that should feature in a whole-school issues mentoring programme. In terms of DfE criteria (1992), the minimum here constitutes the two 'non subject-specific' competences:

- class management
- professional development.

These competences are dealt with in Chapters 5 and 7 respectively. At this stage, however, it's important to stress that mentors could reasonably include other appropriate topics in whole-school issues (and also subject) mentoring. Relevant topics might beneficially include:

- political education/citizenship studies/world studies
- the 'hidden' curriculum
- anti-classist, anti-disablist, anti-racist and anti-sexist initiatives.

These important areas needn't be considered as discrete units: they impinge, though often tacitly, on most of what goes on in schools. At the very least, talk about them during seminars, even if that means flushing them into the open when they might not seem apparent. There will be more about these matters in later chapters. Suffice it to say, at this stage, that you should make space in your timetable for things that don't just feature in DfEE directives.

By extending your whole-school issues brief beyond the official criteria, you'll be able to encourage student teachers to become much more than mere skills instructors. In that context, I urge you to link their practice and their reflection to:

- The goal of promoting social justice through their teaching. It's relevant here to point out that this shouldn't constitute a 'by proxy' exercise: the best starting point for teaching about social justice is to practise it in the classroom.
- The findings of school effectiveness research and how those disclosures might usefully be applied to improve the learning outcomes of school students.

Research into mentoring

On the matter of research, here are some of the skills that Oxford University teacher educators (H. Hagger, K. Burn and D. McIntyre, 1993) found student teachers value in experienced teachers:

- awareness of realities, practicalities, constraints
- classroom control
- dealing with individuals
- knowing when to step in
- opening routines
- building habits with classes
- tried and tested strategies for handling different situations
- knowing how to turn academic knowledge into lesson content that makes sense to the pupils
- timing of a lesson
- different ways of dealing with disruption
- knowing what's going on and how to change tack
- developing ways of interpreting what goes on and being able to respond quickly to classroom events
- marking and assessing
- pitching work appropriately for pupils of different abilities.

Other researchers at Oxford University (S. Rothwell, E. Nardi and D. McIntyre, 1994) found that five mentor activities, in particular, were rated highly valuable by 80 per cent or more of former interns who responded to a questionnaire (response rate: *c.* 60 per cent). To quote directly from this research, these are those much-valued mentor activities:

- Observing interns teaching and providing feedback (95 per cent).
- Discussing with interns teaching methods for their subject (89 per cent).
- Planning individual interns' programmes for teaching and learning, and discussing their progress (82 per cent).
- Discussing with interns lessons they have observed in school (80 per cent).
- Organizing interns' timetables ... (80 per cent).

Additional research (D. Black and M. Booth, 1992) into the views of student teachers on the guidance they received from their mentors revealed that:

- Constructive criticism, in the form of 'non-threatening evaluative feedback', is welcomed. Student teachers need to know how to improve their developing skills, so don't be unhelpfully 'over-protective'.
- Structured opportunities for learning are valued. A hit-and-miss, pick-it-up-as-you-go-along mentoring style won't do.

John Furlong and Trisha Maynard's book *Mentoring Student Teachers* (1995) contains very helpful guidance – based on their research – on how mentors can take student teachers from 'apprentice-style' to 'autonomous' learning. They advise the mentor to:

- Begin 'as a model for the student', providing 'solution-focused' routines 'that can be copied and will actually work in the classroom'.
- Gradually encourage student teachers to become less 'performance-conscious', so that they can '"de-centre" from themselves to the pupils'. The onus here is on getting interns to think, as well as to act, like teachers.
- Give the student teacher the space to become an independent professional who is ready to take more responsibility for her or his learning.

It would certainly be useful if you sought to find out from your own student teachers how best to make explicit and accessible to them the professional/craft skills that are routinely featured in your own teaching. Why not conduct your own research here? I do. Moreover, I use the results to improve those aspects of my mentoring that student teachers report best help them to acquire and develop their teaching and interpersonal skills. Here – based on asking my student teachers how I can assist them most – are some of my findings:

- In the early stages of the school-based programme, let student teachers observe you demonstrating some 'how to do it, real life' drills. 'How to start a lesson' figures prominently here.
- Whenever possible, give student teachers immediate post-lesson debriefings, whether this involves their conferring with you after observing you teaching, or your providing them with constructive feedback after watching them in action.

- Give student teachers the opportunity to do some actual teaching (in measured, supervised and well-selected doses) as early as possible. They're raring to go; tap into that enthusiasm.
- Be fairly explicit in showing student teachers how to use 'pre-emptive strike' strategies that minimise the risk of hitches during lessons: for example, the testing of audio-visual equipment prior to its deployment.

I also sent a questionnaire to 18 mentors who teach in northern England secondary schools, asking them to identify the mentoring knowledge and skills that they believe are most helpful to student teachers. One mentor was approached in each of 14 schools, and four in my own school. Eight mentors returned completed questionnaires, three from my school, and five from five other schools. Their comments are important and insightful. Here are some of them:

'Experience of the changing classroom scene in relation to attitudes and subject demands' (science mentor)

'Help and advice with ... not allowing minor setbacks to destroy morale' (history/social studies mentor)

'Understanding of the department and how it fits into the school as a whole' (history, geography, RE mentor)

'How to tackle problem pupils, how to defuse potential problems, advice on how to cope with stress, cross-curricular issues, and time planning and prioritising' (science mentor)

'ability to advise on and help with job applications, preparing for interviews' (modern foreign languages mentor)

'A real experience of the day-to-day transactions of the classroom. That is, the extent to which the teaching relationship can be typified on a general basis, and to what extent it relies on individual style and relationships' (English mentor)

'Trying to improve perceptions of pupils at differing ability levels' (science mentor)

Moving on to a recent research review of school improvement (P. Sammons, J. Hillman and P. Mortimore, 1995) – the findings of which might usefully be made known to student teachers – among the most important effectiveness factors identified are these:

- purposeful leadership that selects effective teachers, involves them in decision-making and creates common goals and unity

- shared vision and aims which create consistent whole-school policies
- attractive and orderly learning environments that promote self-control among school students
- well-organised, purposeful teaching, appropriately paced and which employs effective questioning to elicit school students' attention
- high expectations and self-esteem among teachers, school students and parents
- positive reinforcement, explicit feedback and rewards and clear disciplinary rules, as opposed to criticism and punishment
- effective and explicit monitoring of school students' progress
- recognition of school students' rights as well as their responsibilities
- home-school partnerships that promote parent support for their children's learning
- an institutional ethos that encourages both staff and school students to improve their performance and keep up with change.

A competence-based model of teacher education

The DfEE is strongly committed to the view that initial teacher education should:

- equip intending teachers with 'the competences necessary for effective practice' (DfE, 1993a)
- ensure that the 'progressive development of these competences [is] monitored regularly during initial training' (DfE, 1992)
- emphasise 'the importance of training being closely linked to its practical application' (DfE, 1993a).

The then DfE (1992) defined the above competences as: subject knowledge, subject application, class management, assessment and recording of pupils' progress, and further professional development. Each of these five headings is subdivided into component parts. For example, class management requires that:

Newly qualified teachers should be able to:

2.4.1   decide when teaching the whole-class, groups, pairs, or individuals is appropriate for particular learning purposes

2.4.2   create and maintain a purposeful and orderly environment for the pupils

2.4.3 devise and use appropriate rewards and sanctions to maintain an effective learning environment

2.4.4 maintain pupils' interest and motivation.

Although the years ahead are likely to witness some adjustments to the DfEE teacher competences – as a result of consultation with providers of accredited courses – the main skills expected of newly qualified teachers are likely to remain broadly as defined in Circular 9/92. After all, most teachers already do and will continue to do what the designated competences make explicit, without feeling the need to refer to DfEE directives.

What teacher doesn't accept that sound subject knowledge is a prerequisite for competent subject application, and that the ability to engage the interest and understanding of school students forms the basis of effective teaching? Are there teachers who don't agree that good class management creates the best environment for favourable behavioural and learning outcomes to flourish? Have you come across teachers who don't believe that the accurate assessment of school students' work is an important predictor of their future progress? And what teacher wouldn't concur that initial teacher education should provide a firm footing for further professional development?

Given then that the DfEE competences provide a useful framework for structuring, in a fairly explicit manner, the learning experiences of intending teachers, this book distils their broad dimensions and provides guidance on how mentors can best help to equip student practitioners with a career-entry repertoire of accredited professional skills. In that respect, by not getting tied down with 'small print' issues, the book focuses on competence domains that are likely to endure even if alterations and amendments are made to specific criteria.

What you, as a mentor, will need to do is keep up with the latest government directives on initial teacher education, and target your mentoring broadly – but not over-prescriptively – in line with the DfEE competences expected of newly qualified teachers. In that context, it's encouraging to note that the DfEE recognises that these competences 'do not purport to provide a complete syllabus' (DfE, 1992).

Moreover, the Government doesn't require mentors to necessarily include, in the career-entry profiles of newly qualified teachers, exhaustive assessments of every single itemised competence. Rather, teacher educators – and here I quote the Teacher Training Agency (1994) – 'should assess professional capabilities and give a picture of relative strengths and weaknesses in areas of competence, citing individual competences within these areas only when they relate to a NQT's (newly qualified teacher's) particular strengths or development needs.'

So don't be too concerned with the overly formulaic aspects of government directives. Stick to the bold outlines, and encourage principled practice.

Notes

Unless defined contexts make particular usages clear, the terms 'school student' and 'student teacher' designate, respectively, persons aged 4–19 attending government maintained schools (popularly referred to as 'state schools') in England and Wales, and persons aged 18 and older attending courses leading to 'newly qualified teacher status' at schools and higher education institutions in England and Wales. To reduce literary tedium, the term 'student teacher' is sometimes used interchangeably with 'intending teacher', 'beginning teacher', and 'intern'.

The term 'classroom' should be interpreted as any school-based learning environment – an actual classroom, a gym, a sportsfield, a science laboratory, a workshop, an information technology suite, etc. – where teaching takes place. 'University' denotes any higher education institute.

Finally, end-of-chapter 'Guidance points' summarise the key issues and directions that mentors should consider.

GUIDANCE POINTS _____

1   Effective mentors help student teachers to become competent classroom teachers, accurate and compassionate assessors of school students' progress, and members of a caring profession.

2   While effective mentoring rightly involves skills instruction, it must also be anchored within a critical and informed theoretical and ethical framework.

3   Mentors need the encouragement and support of senior managers, and the time and the space to practise their craft.

4   Intending mentors should acquire some 'dry-run' practice before starting the real event, preferably under the direction of a professional tutor or an experienced mentor.

5   Mentors need to forge strong links with their co-teacher educators at the university, or, in the case of entirely school-centred initial teacher education courses, with the consortium co-ordinators. There must be a close fit between what happens on campus and what goes on at school.

6   It's important that mentors obtain as much background information as possible on the student teachers they'll be working with. Mentors should also send student teachers relevant details about the school and the department(s), and a prospective, but negotiable, timetable.

7   Student teachers should be invited to a pre-placement induction day (or

days) at the school, when they should be briefed on their forthcoming programme and consulted on a timetable that contains: first and second subject teaching (solo and co-teaching included); a weekly tutorial with the mentor; on-site 'training' (especially computer applications); and non-contact time.

8 Mentors must provide intending teachers with opportunities to observe and gain experience in both subject teaching and whole-school issues work. It's also essential that student teachers are assisted to relearn their subject knowledge in a manner that both targets school syllabuses and makes it accessible to school students of varying abilities.

9 Research shows that, among other skills, student teachers want mentors to help them become adept at making the complex simple, and properly equipped to handle disruptive behaviour ('pre-emptive strike' tips are especially welcomed). They also like mentors to provide: non-threatening, honest feedback on their progress; drill-style demonstrations of key teacher strategies (e.g. how to 'settle' a class); and fairly early chances to 'have a go' at real teaching, but in measured, initially supervised, doses.

CHAPTER 2

Teachers teaching teachers

In a speech to the North of England Education Conference on 4 January 1992, the then Secretary of State, Kenneth Clarke, rebuked the 'orthodoxies of the past' for allegedly making initial teacher education courses so harmfully impractical. In responding to this alleged problem, the Government declared its intention to severely trim an excess of educational theory by requiring intending teachers to spend much more time in schools under the watchful eye of serving teachers.

A new Secretary of State, John Patten (since replaced, in 1994, by Gillian Shephard) announced in June 1992 that his predecessor's proposal would become official policy so far as the 'training' of secondary school teachers was concerned. Mr Patten's decision was set out in DfE Circular 9/92, which gave:

- schools a pivotal role in initial teacher education, and the funding to support this new responsibility
- more time in schools for student teachers

- an emphasis on the 'training' of student teachers in essential competences.

A parallel document, DfE Circular 14/93, was issued by Mr Patten in 1993, providing similar reforms for the initial teacher education of primary school teachers. In that same year, the Education Secretary also announced the introduction of a pilot scheme, whereby selected schools in consortia would receive £4000 for each student teacher they enrolled, and be enabled, if they chose, to provide the entire pre-service programme. So enthusiastic was the Government about this new venture that school-centred 'training' became 'treated in the Green Paper in which it was mooted as a success before it had begun ...' (T. Edwards, 1994).

The Government's backing of the school consortium model hasn't, however, resulted in a takeover by schools of what the universities do in initial teacher education. The vast majority of schools haven't decided to become the sole educators of intending teachers. The partnership model, whereby mentors take care of the school side of things and university tutors provide student teachers with the opportunity to consider educational debates and the insights of research, is a much more popular option.

I don't believe this division of labour should be pushed too far, though. Increasingly and beneficially, mentors encourage reflective practice and engage in school-based research (often with university guidance), and some of their campus-based counterparts are returning to the 'chalkface'. The University of London's Institute of Education, for example, sends its academics back into schools to ensure they don't lose touch with events in modern classrooms.

Perhaps there's a need for a radically different type of teacher educator, one who is, to quote Frank Murray (1995), 'as equally at home in a school as in the university'. Whether or not such a new-style faculty member ever arrives on the scene, partnerships between schools and universities look set to stay. However, things have changed since the days when school teachers, compared to university tutors, played a 'subsidiary' role in initial teacher education.

Partners in teacher education

Until very recently, schools were 'simply places to which student teachers have been sent for "teaching practice"' (H. Hagger, K. Burn and D. McIntyre, 1993). DfE Circular 9/92 changed all that. The Circular announced the Government's plan of making the initial teacher education of intending secondary teachers predominantly school-based.

Specifically, the minimum time student teachers are to spend in partner schools is:

- in full-time secondary PGCE courses, 24 weeks
- in full-time four-year secondary undergraduate courses, 32 weeks
- in full-time two- and three-year secondary undergraduate courses, 24 weeks.

The ratio of PGCE to undergraduate students on secondary courses is about three to one. This means that the majority of secondary student teachers receive about two-thirds of their initial teacher education on school premises. Whether you work with postgraduate or undergraduate student teachers, you, the mentor, will have the main responsibility for – not delegated supervision of – the school-based parts of the course. Moreover, your partner teacher educator, the university tutor, will be expected to provide intending teachers with a campus programme that is directly relevant to what goes on in schools.

So what does this imply for that enduring debate about theory and practice, about the allegedly idealised concerns of campus educators and the gritty realities faced by the mentor?

Idealism, reality, or both?

Some student teachers expect their mentors to replace theoretical reflection with practical strategies. This is perhaps an understandable but a regrettable assumption. After all, what mentor wants to train an intending teacher to be 'streetwise smart', yet unconcerned with reflective practice?

However, the different work situations of tutors and mentors give some student teachers the impression that the respective roles of their co-educators are at odds with each other. Tutors are able and expected to theorise; mentors are better placed to deal with real events. At least, that's how the argument runs. I don't agree. While a certain division of labour is inevitable and helpful, tutors and mentors are both involved in the educating of future teachers.

With this common goal in mind, it's vital that both parties work to a com-mon agenda to ensure there's a spin off from what is presented and discussed on campus and what is practised at school. Moreover, it's better for student teachers to study in detail a few theories that connect with classroom improvement strategies than to encounter what Ed Stones (1993) describes as 'the ritualistic gallop through the gurus from Plato to Piaget in ten lectures'.

So be sure, in co-operation with campus-based teacher educators, to forge strong and relevant theory–practice connections. In that context, I think it's a good idea to leave the 'theory versus practice' debate to abstract philosophers (no disrespect intended, but this book can't hope to settle that interminable polemic), and to realise that the relationship between these two domains is often more artificial than real.

When, for example, as a teacher, I provide my school students with stretching but achievable learning tasks, I know that the theories which derive from educational research (itself a practical venture) support this strategy as an example of good practice. In terms, then, of the principles that underpin my teaching, theory and practice bounce off each other. Antipathy among student teachers towards theory is more likely to be apparent when there are obvious discontinuities between what's theorised and what's actually possible.

That said, student teachers shouldn't surrender their ideals to the exigencies of so-called 'practical realities'. Pitting 'theory as idealism' against 'practice as pragmatism' is disingenuous, as well as unprincipled. Where would teaching be if teachers didn't have ideals? It's true that institutional structures sometimes make it hard for teachers to practise what they believe, but being aware of that potential tension can increase the resolve of teachers to place decency before the easy option. Indeed, as Donald McIntyre (1990) rightly observes, student teachers 'should be aware of the necessary tensions between … theoretical conceptions and the various practical and selfish concerns of those concerned with schooling …'.

Provided there's a tight fit between ideal models and achievable goals, there's absolutely no need to pit theory and practice against each other. But mentors and teachers have to work hard to obtain that fit, and, with this goal in mind, they shouldn't be side-tracked into imagining that DfEE competence directives are only concerned with practical issues. While the official discourse doesn't go far enough to promote a full consideration of the crucial link between critical reflection and purposeful action, it nevertheless contains sufficient scope to make theories of learning and educational achievement important features of effective mentoring. In that spirit, it's salutary to note John Furlong's (1995a) observation, that the people who drafted Circular 9/92:

> have to some degree recognised the importance of addressing more than mere behavioural skills. Students are also expected to 'understand' the school as an institution; to 'judge' pupil performance; to have an 'awareness' of individual differences …. A narrowly mechanistic approach to initial teacher education is not demanded by this Circular. If that is the result it will be because we have imposed it on ourselves.

Don't treat DfE Circular 9/92 (and any subsequent amendment) too narrowly. Exercise levity, and avoid getting pinned down in the small print. I think you'll find that this is the view adopted by your co-teacher educators on campus, but do get together and come up with a shared agenda.

Mentoring as professional development

On the subject of campus counterparts, it's pertinent to recognise that their redefined role as partners (with us) in initial teacher education has profound implications for the professional development of mentors. There's considerably more scope than previously for outstanding classroom teachers to gain 'privileged status recognition' for what must count as the most important teaching skill – getting it right at the sharp end – as well as moving professionally forward as, first, a career mentor, and, later, a professional tutor.

For some colleagues, becoming a professional tutor (in my school, defined as a co-ordinator of school-based initial teacher education and a manager of staff professional development) is a career destination – and a very important and senior one at that. For other colleagues, a professional tutor post, after some several years in the job, serves as a platform for promotion to a deputy headship, and later a headship. Indeed, I think we can all look forward to an increase in the recruitment of 'class-teacher friendly' and 'class-teacher competent' headteachers, as more and more mentors move into senior management positions. That must be a good thing.

Other career moves include:

- research and teaching in university-based teacher education courses (most professors of education were once school teachers, and, probably, teaching practice supervisors)
- advisory and inspectorate posts (local authority and OFSTED), especially on the 'quality control' side of accredited teacher education courses.

But let's not forget those important colleagues of our number who decide that mentoring is where they want to stay. They have a hugely important role in making their hard-won professional expertise available to student teachers, not just for imitation but also for scrutiny and reflection. What they're offering is much more than a basic 'survival kit' to the intending teacher. They're also reminding those who would be teachers that teaching isn't just a skill, it's a reflective and an ethically infused skill. As the next chapter argues, effective mentors are exponents of intelligent and compassionate practice.

GUIDANCE POINTS _____

1   Good mentors see idealism and realism in teaching as complementary, not opposites.

2   Educational theories that connect with real school issues should be emphasised.

3   DfEE directives contain sufficient scope to go beyond the mere practicalities of teaching.

4   Mentoring is an important avenue of professional development, especially for teachers who want to gain promotion while still remaining in the classroom.

5   Mentors' craft/professional skills aren't just for imitation, they should also be scrutinised.

CHAPTER 3

Principled mentoring

Mentors are expected to provide intending teachers with access to expert practical knowledge. This task is defined by the DfEE expectation that 'training' should 'equip students with essential "competences", including the subject knowledge and professional and personal skills which new teachers need to manage, maintain order and teach effectively in their classrooms' (DfE, 1993a).

The emphasis on linking 'training' to competences is understood by mentors. But, by themselves, the technical criteria of the DfEE sit uneasily on mentors who aspire to be more than just 'trainers', who want to help student teachers acquire the pedagogical and moral leverage to become principled, as well as competent, practitioners.

That's why the education of intending teachers requires an initiation into an explicitly defined body of professional skills that have a moral and 'political' (wider society, rather than party political) purpose. In that sense, student teachers should be encouraged to:

● critically examine, with the guidance and support of tutors and mentors, the competences that 'are designed to ensure that new entrants to the teaching profession are well equipped for their role' (DfE, 1993a)
● model their practice on the ways in which mentors successfully demonstrate competences, and critically discuss with mentors the wider moral and political issues in which educational practice is embedded.

While the university side of initial teacher education is briefly considered in this chapter, the principal focus is on encouraging student teachers to learn and cultivate their skills and act compassionately in the school. For the school is where I do my work; it's also the place where I emphasise to student teachers that their intended profession demands both practical strategies and principled aims.

But how do I define 'principled'? I believe that principled teaching begins with the work teachers do on a day-to-day basis. It has more to do with acting out one's authentic humanity than with talking about human rights in an abstract way. The American educationist Jonathan Kozol (1993) eloquently describes the kind of humanity I have in mind, when he writes:

> I listen to the voices of extraordinary people with a deep tradition of persistence in the face of system-wide timidity and intimidation – teachers who have worked from day to day, and year to year, with neither the glamour of book publication nor the short-lived glow of press or media attention, seldom rewarded in any way at all except perhaps in the one and only way that decent teachers ever find reward: in the gratification of a difficult job well done and in a very basic kind of private dignity courageously upheld.

For me, upholding that 'basic kind of private dignity' with courage and perseverance, even when a school's institutional culture or the values of the wider community might have a different agenda, is what lies at the heart of principled teaching. How, for example, should a newly qualified teacher who believes in treating school students with courtesy and dignity behave if advised by senior staff to be openly 'kind' only when they've frightened the school students into submission? My reply to that question is, 'Reject the advice; it's not only unethical, it's also a case of "received wisdom" running ahead of actual evidence'.

But I don't presume to have access to a better understanding of what's right and wrong than you, the reader. Perhaps you agree with my concept of 'principled'; perhaps not. So where do we go from here? I maintain that a principled teacher is one who acts on conscience whether or not this coincides with a particular institution or system. Making my conscience explicit, I believe that principled teaching is characterised by an endeavour by the teacher to:

- Enhance the life chances of school students by providing them – all of them – with opportunities to maximise their credentialised learning outcomes. Students who leave school without qualifications in the neighbourhood where I teach face low-paid work at best, and unemployment at worst. If my former school students are a pay packet or a welfare cheque away from poverty, I'm not doing my job well.

    To stop that happening, I'm seeking, with some success, to set up 'shared gatekeeping' roles between school teachers and university admissions tutors designed to give socially disadvantaged school students a more realistic chance of entering university. We teachers must persuade these admissions tutors that it's hypocritical to use principled rhetoric in lecture halls if they don't give less qualified school-leavers a realistic prospect of entering higher education. In that context, I think it's vital that the universities do much more in terms of providing 'basic skills' induction programmes for these prospective undergraduates.

- Make the 'hidden curriculum' explicit, especially those aspects of it that demean the dignity and diminish the opportunities of school students who are underachieving relative to their real potential. I particularly have in mind: girls who don't get the teacher time they deserve; black and Asian students whose history doesn't figure in entrance foyers and on wall displays; students who are disabled and who don't receive the support they need; and working-class students who are made to feel that they should leave their culture at the school gate.

    My first subject specialism, sociology, is an emancipatory discipline, and it allows me to make these damaging aspects of the hidden curriculum explicit through classroom discussion and debate. Moreover, my department's mission statement, issued to all social sciences students and to all student teachers with whom I work as a subject mentor, makes it clear that racism, sexism, and all the other negative '-isms' are things that must be challenged.

- Be kind and courteous to their school students. In practical terms, this means challenging the much-touted maxim referred to earlier of starting out tough (read, 'frighten your school students into obedience') and easing up later (read, 'lighten up if school students become sufficiently acquiescent'). There's something horribly insincere about acting on that maxim: it puts practicality before decency.

    I urge my student teachers not to emulate teachers who use cruel and unusual punishments, and who bark discourteous orders at children in classrooms and corridors. Aside from the better behaviour and learning that issue when teachers relate to school students in an atmosphere distinguished by its generosity of spirit, principled teachers are excellent role models.

The above examples of 'principled teaching in practice' don't, of course, constitute an exhaustive list. They encapsulate, in the context of my own professional work, what I value and what I seek to achieve. It's very important, though, to emphasise that if the teacher and the system are in harmony, there's no moral tension. It's when the opposite occurs that teachers are faced with a painful choice: to do what they believe to be right even if that means challenging the organisational ethos, or to surrender their principles and become uncritical servants of the wider structure.

Having made my own private morality public, it's now relevant to provide more background information on the institutional and neighbourhood cultures which impinge upon my mentoring work. While your professional environment undoubtedly differs from mine in certain respects, we both do the same kind of work.

The background to my work

As indicated in the first chapter, I'm head of social sciences at an 11–19, 1800-roll comprehensive school in the north of England, where I teach A level sociology and Key Stage 3 history. I work alongside a colleague who teaches A level law and two colleagues who teach A level psychology. During the 1993–4 school year, I was a subject mentor to three PGCE students from the University of York during their first and last placements of the one-year course. Two students specialised in business studies and economics, and one in history. In the second term, I was a subject mentor to a sociology and to a history student teacher for their main placement. The business studies and economics and history students spent most of their classroom time in the departments that teach those subjects; the sociology student honed his skills in my department. All five students met with me for a 70-minute reflective seminar on a weekly basis. That doesn't mean that we weren't reflective at other times. However, the sharp-end pace of working in a large, busy comprehensive school makes it hard to adopt a leisurely 'stand back and ponder it' stance.

From the beginning of the 1994–5 school year, my mentoring role changed in certain respects. In addition to continuing my subject mentoring, I also assisted in the whole-school issues mentoring of 15 PGCE students from the same university during the first and third terms. They comprised two English specialists, two modern languages specialists, eight science specialists and two history specialists. My work in whole-school issues mentoring has already been described in Chapter 1, and doesn't require further explanation here. As for my subject mentor role, I also mentored two sociology student teachers during the second term (main placement) of the 1994–5 school year.

The catchment area

My school is purpose-built and is located in a predominantly urban, white, working-class neighbourhood on the outskirts of the city. The area's coal-mining heritage is proudly proclaimed by a school tapestry of a coal-seamed underbelly. Coal-mining has recently started again, about a mile or so from the school. But it's now attracting local opposition because it's of the open-cast, rather than the former deep mine type, and, presumably, causes more obvious impact.

The school admits students from the immediate neighbourhood and from outlying districts, including one of the poorest areas of the city, where, curiously, uncarpeted dwellings and satellite dishes co-exist. When people are unemployed – as many of them are in this former mining area – watching television makes a bleak, hard life just a little more bearable. In the immediate

27

vicinity of the school, today's inhabitants are mainly of 'new working class' stock, more likely to be found in service occupations than in heavy industry. However, there's still a blue-collar feel about the community, reflected in part by the school brass band and the local working men's club. Some managerial and professional families reside in the area on private estates and in semi-detached houses. Not so their less well-paid neighbours, who generally occupy council estates and two-up, two-down terraces. It's from these families, pre-dominantly urban working class with some clusters of salaried employees, that most of our students come.

The school ethos

Inasmuch as the cultures of the school and the local community coincide, I think that parents, governors and senior staff want the school to provide a learning and a pastoral environment that encourages:

- a high level of conforming behaviour
- tough discipline: if not self-, then staff-imposed
- a strict dress code: uniform is compulsory up to Year 11
- good public examination results
- access to higher education
- little or no truancy
- regular, rigorously monitored homework
- success in sporting events.

Although there's a measure of 'sub-cultural resistance' among certain 'progressive' teachers to this 'official' ethos, there's quite a lot of organisational pressure on teachers not to be too effusive in their protestations. In fact, faced with recalcitrant students during tough substitution periods, it's sometimes convenient to take the line of least resistance by invoking the threat of punishment.

Going with the flow – in this case an authoritarian current – is easy because students are socialised into a tightly 'policed' system. Most students give in without manifest protestation; a sizeable minority make token protests but yield quickly when teachers get tough; a very small number accomplish those more subtle forms of institutional rebellion so vividly captured by the sociologist Paul Willis (1988), namely the sustaining of 'an aimless air of insubordination ready with spurious justification and impossible to nail down'.

Yet survival, from an 'I'm in charge' angle, isn't hard to achieve where punitive back-up is readily available. Even the toughest school students can usually be brought into line through quite severe punishments, should initial actions fail to elicit appropriate submissiveness. But where does all this lead? Measured against DfEE criteria, the tough disciplinarians score highly on the criteria used for 'competent' class managers. How do they fare, though, on the unofficial but very important scale of being principled in their work? I can't answer that question for them. But it's my view that teachers who use sanctions pragmatically, without considering the wider ethical and political implications of punishment, aren't coming to grips with ethical practice.

As a teacher and as a mentor, it's my task to find ways to act on my belief in non-combative styles of class management and to make that expertise available to student teachers in a regime strongly buttressed by a system of sanctions. Yet theirs is a very different educational setting. When they come to me, they exchange a tolerant, tree-lined campus in the cathedral city of York some twenty-five miles away to enter a much hardier environment.

Institutional cultures

This contrast of environments – the one urbane, the other gritty – is to some extent complemented by differing institutional cultures. The campus is able to cultivate a reflective ethos; the school has to focus on practicalities. This produces a tension: university tutors encourage student teachers to step outside of and reflect upon the context of mere doing; school mentors offer the distilled wisdom of 'intelligent practical knowledge'.

There's something inevitable about this. Universities don't have school students on site. That gives campus tutors the space and the time to encourage student teachers to debate the promises and the limitations of scripted classroom strategies. Mentors, by contrast, are dispensers of 'know-how' in classrooms, gyms, sportsfields, corridors and canteens, and, by DfEE decree, assessors of the developing competences of student teachers in the school.

In that respect, James Calderhead (1992) is probably right when he claims that 'in schools a much higher priority is given to immediate, spontaneous action rather than analysis and reflection'. Schools are geared to practical concerns. Moreover, some student teachers expect their mentors to give 'off-the-shelf' guidance rather than vaguely felt musings.

However, mentors shouldn't limit their counsel to a list of 'teacher should ...' directives. It's also important to consider issues that go beyond the learning outcome audits prescribed by DfEE chiefs, like how important it is to let school students display righteous anger during a heated classroom debate, instead of automatically invoking what the DfEE refers to as 'appropriate sanctions'. In that spirit, my co-teacher educators at the university accept that, while there's a necessary division of labour between mentors and tutors, what happens in schools is much more than just 'shooting from the hip'. Good teachers are contemplative practitioners.

Granted, given the practical setting in which I work, I try to translate the minutiae of DfEE legalese into broad descriptions and practical strategies. But student teachers need to know that being a teacher means more than successfully demonstrating an inventory of pre-specified competences. If competences are over-emphasised, mentors risk turning out the kind of newly qualified teacher who, as David Carr (1993) says, 'may perform routinely well according to the behest of others rather than on the basis of her own principled understanding'.

Class-management styles

I'll illustrate this point with reference to some actual mentoring: specifically, how I respond, in work with student teachers, to the DfEE competence criteria on class management. The official criteria use the language of control: 'decide when', 'create', 'devise and use', 'maintain'. There are also references to 'orderly environments' and 'appropriate rewards and sanctions'. Such state-mandated vocabulary isn't at odds with what my school expects of its teachers. But it doesn't coincide with my conception of principled teaching and principled mentoring.

In seminars with my student teachers, I ask them to consider the extent to which their own beliefs align with the official agenda of DfEE directives and school practice. But this doesn't mean substituting whimsical diversions for the real business of getting these intending teachers properly prepared for work in the classroom. Like me, they know that they must display competence in making complex tasks achievable for all their students, in utilising individual, group and whole-class teaching to good effect, and in taking account of psychological and social factors in the assessment of learning outcomes.

These skills are 'permitted' by DfE Circular 9/92, and they demand prior reflection and discussion. Moreover, such competences aren't reducible to a scripted list of behavioural reponses. Competent teachers are contextual experts. They've become adept at identifying particular cues – the procedural discipline of the science laboratory, the impromptu incident in the playground – and at, almost effortlessly, it seems, taking the appropriate course of action. Competent teachers also look beyond the immediacy of the next lesson. In that sense, they apply competences thoughtfully and relevantly, and plan ahead.

When mentors open up what they do so routinely and so effectively in schools to student teachers, they need to make receptiveness to background contingencies and long-term strategies clear. This might mean, for example, explaining that regional dialects in the classroom shouldn't be considered inferior to so-called Standard English. In that context, it would be relevant to point out that social scientific research documents the damaging effects upon self-esteem and learning outcomes when school students are made to feel that their culture (of which a dialect is an important part) isn't welcomed in the classroom. There's the important issue here too of encouraging intending teachers to adopt a principled attitude: of showing that they respect and welcome cultural diversity.

It's also relevant, during discussions between mentors and student teachers, to consider and debate the relative merits of different class-management styles. At the two extremes are autocratic rule and collective decision-making. In between are varying degrees of control and facilitative strategies. Student teachers need to know that some teachers are selective, employing the method that, in their judgement, best fits a particular circumstance, while others are predominantly autocratic or consultative, whatever the situation. From a principled standpoint, it's essential to take the discussion into wider political and ethical domains. Is it the proper role of the teacher in society to frighten children into bowing to an adult point of view? Is it morally acceptable for the teacher to 'lay down the law' in the classroom rather than to invite meaningful dialogue? These are important questions. They mustn't be side-stepped. Nor should mentors urge pragmatism by using expressions like 'It's wrong to use intimidation, but, in practice, you must stamp your authority rather forcefully, easing off when students start showing you respect.' Raw power is never respected; authority, which has to be earned, is.

Conversely, it's important to recognise that class management shouldn't be totally non-directive. In terms of real benefits to school students – measured in learning outcomes and the growth of respect for deserved authority – teachers do need to manage and they do need to teach. Otherwise, they run the risk, to quote Jonathan Kozol (1993), 'of thinking that a minimum of hard work and a maximum of whimsical diversion will prove the perfect formula for student adulation'.

I make sure my student teachers get to watch traditionalist and progressive class managers. Sometimes subject cultures are at work here: PE teachers are usually more directive, for very good reasons, than humanities teachers. There are also ethical factors: some teachers believe that tough discipline is good for children; others advocate a gentler approach. There are conviction teachers in both camps. But it's not for me to tell student teachers that persuaders are better people than disciplinarians – or vice versa. Principled practitioners come in different shapes and sizes. What they have in common is a passionate concern for the education and the well-being of their school students.

So in your selection of 'role model' class managers for student teachers to watch and, if possible, to work alongside, provide a wide variety of management styles: the personal and social education teacher who cheers when a school student throws a spitball in defence of a spirited idea, as well as the CDT teacher who upholds a strict code of health and safety practices in the metal workshop. I think it's important too that student teachers are able to meet teachers who 'allow' their school students to stand by what they believe in, even if that means saying 'No' in the company of a teacher. For there are different ways of saying 'No'. There's the refusal based on the honest rebuttal of an idea, and the refusal that malevolently attacks the authority of a teacher. Principled teachers know this distinction.

It's also necessary to give student teachers the chance to observe and to try their hand at those aspects of class management that require even the most 'progressive' of teachers to take a lead in their dealings with school students. Bearing in mind that classes don't just occupy classrooms, but also move around the school, I extend this 'look and have a go' exercise to corridors and bus bays, both of which require adult supervision.

At the same time, I emphasise, in discussion and – I hope – by example, that class management, from both a principled and an effective standpoint, should be non-coercive. Conscientious mentors who sense that the DfEE wants them to turn out 'carrot and stick' class managers are faced with a difficult choice: to preach and practise 'boss management', or to advocate and adopt a non-custodial style.

I prefer the second of these two options. Not only do I tell my student teachers that this approach allows me to remain honest to my beliefs, I also point out that my professional work and the findings of important research (e.g. DES, 1989) suggest it's a style that works well in real classroom situations. In short, my approach isn't just a personal ethical stand; it's grounded in experience and supported by evidence.

But does the institutional culture of the school permit the same degree of humanity as the more detached, progressive ethos of the university? Unlike myself, tutors don't have to contend with the 'Don't mess with me' outlook of certain senior teachers who maintain that showing compassion towards 'difficult' school students displays weakness rather than decency. Such an outlook can easily become the dominant control culture of a school, especially if it's actively promoted by senior managers. This view can also lend credence to that dangerous juxtaposition which suggests that schools deal with real issues and universities merely speculate.

Teachers must resist organisational pressures to conform to beliefs and practices which they believe are wrong. It's important, though, to engage in resistance that neither rebukes custodial-minded colleagues, nor confuses students with avant-garde messages that are out of harmony with a formal regime. Discussing this tension with student teachers is part of the process of encouraging reflective practice.

Teachers are reflective too

These days it's common for academics to urge school teachers to become reflective practitioners. One detects, in this admonition, an assumption on the part of our campus counterparts that we teachers are so overwhelmed by contemporary pressures that we've lost our idealism. I hope that this is not the case. There are still teachers, schools and education authorities who conscientiously struggle against prejudice and injustice, who strive to give all their students an educational and an ethical preparation for the world in and beyond the classroom. When, for example, education authorities like my own, Leeds City Council, produce written policies on equal opportunities, teachers are expected to reflect on the implications, as well as acting on the principles, of such initiatives.

Illustrative of that point, I recently invited two council officials who have a special interest in women's issues into my classroom. They explained to my class and me how routine practices in schools are often gendered in ways that work against girls and women. Their presentations elicited a lot of critical discussion and have encouraged us to recognise and challenge sexism.

I've also spoken to other teachers in my school about the ways in which they have consistently developed practical strategies, premised on a great deal of constructive reflection, for confronting gendered prejudices and for helping students to eradicate sexist assumptions from their daily lives.

Moreover, my department's mission statement, referred to earlier, states clearly where I and my colleagues stand on issues that are crucially linked to principled professional practice. For example, the document makes it clear that the department is committed to:

> Encouraging and enabling you (the school student) to base your studies and your moral and citizenship outlook on objective, anti-ageist, anti-racist and anti-sexist criteria. If we (the teachers) manage to replace any negative 'ism' with an enlightened, generous outlook, any hearsay judgement with critical awareness, any half-truth with honest scholarship, then we will have done our job well.

Statements like this aren't designed to produce knee-jerk responses to unexpected events; rather the opposite. Their purpose is to promote critical reflection and responsible learning and teaching. Moreover, the above statement didn't just jump onto a page. It was considered, discussed, refined and eventually written with a long-term goal in mind: to cultivate in our school students an ability and a readiness to identify and challenge those attitudes and practices in society that undermine equality and social justice.

Practitioner research

Further indicative of reflective work on the part of teachers is the growth of practitioner-led research in schools, often linked to school improvement programmes. In this area, I've initiated research into those aspects of initial teacher education that student teachers report are of most help to them in acquiring and augmenting class-management skills. This research involves collaboration with academics at the university, who provide expert guidance on methods and data interpretation.

But the project is conducted by two teachers, myself and a colleague, who are crossing the traditional divide between 'chalkface' and campus cultures. Not only are we engaged in reflective research whose findings will, hopefully, help to turn out good class managers, we're also getting our student teachers to do a lot of hard reflecting. Out of a series of informal interviews and some questionnaires, important and interesting findings are emerging.

Student teachers, in our case study, report that class-management styles are:

- best introduced and considered on campus prior to school placement, through the use of videos, role-play, and seminar-style discussion
- very effectively learnt, before experience-based autonomy develops, through the observation of skilled teachers who put on 'going through the motions' demonstrations that are accompanied by follow-up discussions and 'have a go' practice
- quite clearly linked to specific subjects (more emphasis on hierarchical command structures is deemed necessary in technology practicals, for example, than in discursive humanities classes)
- closely related to overarching institutional cultures (my school is seen as tough on discipline, and student teachers feel they're expected to fall in line with that ethos, whether or not this accords with their own ethical style).

Although the research is suggestive rather than representative, it tentatively questions the notion that class management is simply a technical skill whose accomplishment can be developed by copying mentor models. To be sure, that aspect plays an important part – especially in the early stages. Yet student teachers see a need too for reflective work and for discussions about how their private moralities interact with DfEE and public expectations regarding the teacher's role as disciplinarian.

Principled practice

They also need the chance to engage in principled practice during initial teacher education. I know this might seem rather idealistic, given that some colleagues tell student teachers that school students deal 'soft-touch beginners' a tough hand. Yet, in my experience, most school students respond affably and productively when they recognise fair-mindedness in their teachers. In that spirit, and supported by the evidence of my own practitioner research, as well as by the published research of university academics (e.g. S. Brown and D. McIntyre, 1993; E. C. Wragg, 1993), I advise student teachers, for ethical and practical reasons, to demonstrate qualities that school students say they appreciate:

- displaying a sense of humour without being ridiculously jolly
- avoiding condescending remarks and rebuffs
- showing patience when a class or an individual gets stuck
- demonstrating that they know their subject well
- having enthusiasm for their subject
- being caring, kind and sympathetic
- making complex issues accessible
- adopting measured firmness if things get out of hand
- maintaining fairness and integrity when adjudicating disputes.

In dispensing this counsel, I acknowledge that my student teachers are becoming not just exponents of a craft, but members of a caring profession. They need competences and moral purpose. I think the DfEE puts too much emphasis on the skills side of things; yet a careful reading of its criteria reveals that a sensitivity to the differing learning and personal needs of school students is also necessary. Would that the DfEE gave such pastoral awareness more of an explicit focus. But that shouldn't discourage mentors from emphasising the caring work upon which principled practice is based.

Campus educators use lectures, seminars, tutorials and workshops to deal with the ethics and the politics of the teacher's role. We mentors employ some of those methods, but we also contextualise the debate in professional practice. In that respect, I find one of the best ways to make student teachers aware that this authentic labour has both reflective and craft dimensions is to move the school-based experiences of student teachers beyond the routines of classrooms, corridors and gym halls into the decision-making arenas that are also an integral part of school life.

A good way to do this is to have student teachers shadow experienced teachers at heads of department, staff, and governors' meetings. These events provide important opportunities to observe vigorous debates that throw into relief the harmonies and the tensions which emerge when individuals and social structures lock horns on ethical and political matters. They're social encounters that shouldn't be off bounds to intending teachers because they create agendas which evoke a great deal of reflection. In that respect, they also remind teachers that what goes on in schools isn't confined to checklists of competences.

For that's the risk engendered in a preoccupation with the identification and assessment of officially defined criteria. Put simply, there are some qualities in the making of good teachers that can't be squeezed into a competence profile. Indeed, as Ian Davies and Ernesto Macaro (1995) so rightly remark: 'It would be possible for a student to do well against all competence statements and yet still be regarded as a poor teacher.'

There's something about principled practice that doesn't square with just 'learning the ropes'. No mentor wants to help create a teacher who knows how to put on an ethical show but who isn't moved by a conscientious desire to put compassion above organisational imperatives. The humanitarian mentor fosters the very qualities that coercive school regimes ignore: always being courteous; starting out and staying kind; highlighting and challenging any institutional arrangements that obstruct equal opportunities for black students, students who are disabled, female students and working-class students.

With these ends in mind, mentors need to supplement their advice on how to accomplish DfEE-prescribed competences with independent and creative discussions on the nature and the practice of principled teaching. Only then will we be able to help tomorrow's teachers to develop that ingenuity and conviction which enables them to do much more than be merely competent. We will assist them in becoming professionals who take the time to care about what they do and, above all, who make the decision to care about their students.

In this chapter, I've argued that competence-led initial teacher education shouldn't be separated from the consideration and practice of principled teaching. I've also suggested that student teachers should critically examine the ways in which their professional duties are defined by institutional arrangements. Where there's harmony of moral and political purpose between the individual and the school, this represents an almost perfect situation. But where this isn't so, mentors need to show intending teachers, through reflective discussion and just practice, that there's a principled way forward.

The socialisation of intending and newly qualified teachers into a professional teaching culture needn't be at odds with the idealism more usually associated with campus culture. As David Bridges (1995) asserts, there's a place in teacher education programmes (both pre-service and in-service) for:

> the development of moral schemata and wider socio-political frameworks of thinking without which teachers will fall prey to the lowest forms of unquestioning pragmatism and lose that personal integrity without which they are scarcely entitled to invite the trust and confidence of their students.

It's certainly important to realise that there's no inevitability of a 'wash-out' effect, whereby mentors purge compassion and replace it with 'bareknuckle realism'. For what's real can and should be founded on moral and political purpose. Many of my professional colleagues know and live by that belief. Some of them, to be sure, are forced to fight for their idealism when, for example, they work in schools where enterprise culture seeks to hijack a commitment to public service. But, ultimately, teachers must take responsibility for the normative structures in which they do their work. They shouldn't surrender to a system in which they don't believe. Instead, with like-minded colleagues and through their own professional practice, they should seek to change the system. Principled practice demands this.

GUIDANCE POINTS _____

1   Mentors should help student teachers to become both competent and principled members of their intended profession.

2   Initial teacher education doesn't take place in a moral and political vacuum: the moral and political role of teachers in society must be faced up to.

3   Social justice begins with what teachers do, not with what they preach.

4   Being 'principled' means doing what's right in preference to institutional 'cheap shots'; conviction should be celebrated, not regarded as unrealistic.

5   Mission statements flush the potentially harmful effects of the 'hidden curriculum' into the open, and enable them to be openly challenged.

6   Mentors shouldn't tout the largely anecdotal belief that student teachers need to start off tough. Research findings show that being consistently kind and fair-minded produces better outcomes: it's also morally right to behave that way.

7   Mentors and university tutors need to encourage reflective practice if the perceived boundary between 'campus idealism' and 'chalkface reality' is to be broken down.

8   DfEE competence criteria shouldn't be treated too literally; mentors should interpret 'official initial teacher education syllabuses' flexibly, and recognise that they're not all-embracing.

9   The 'wash out' effect, whereby visionary aspirations become overwhelmed by practicalities, is only inevitable if student teachers are persuaded to compromise their authentic humanity. It's up to mentors to keep idealism alive.

CHAPTER 4

Essential mentoring skills

Whatever you teach and whether you're a subject mentor, a whole-school issues mentor, or both, there are important generic skills that underpin all effective mentoring. These skills – which often overlap – are:

- planning
- liaising
- demonstrating
- facilitating
- observing
- assessing
- guiding.

Some areas of mentoring make more or less use of the above techniques than others. This chapter considers and provides professionally grounded advice on each of the skills under their separate headings, mainly but not exclusively in the context of class teaching.

Planning

In my school, the planning that initiates:

- the designation and deployment of mentors
- the number of student teachers admitted to school placements
- the amount paid by the university to the school per student teacher for the provision of mentoring (£1200 annually for each student teacher in my school)
- how that money is allocated once it's in the school coffers

begins in negotiations between senior teachers (notably a deputy headteacher, a professional tutor, and five heads of department; three of these five are mentors) and senior university staff (notably the head of educational studies and the director of the PGCE course).

It's important that your voice gets heard and acted upon at all levels of the planning stage. After all, it's you, the mentor, who is at the cutting edge of the whole operation. Moreover, it's appropriate for mentors to play a role in the selection process of prospective entrants to initial teacher education courses. This 'sharing of the gatekeeping' between chalkface and campus teacher educators is already happening in a number of partnership schemes across the country. I hope it's a development that will flourish, now that teachers are playing a far more proactive role than hitherto in teacher education programmes.

Once the above arrangements have been finalised, it's time to plan for the arrival of student teachers in the school. This aspect of planning has already been considered in Chapter 1, so there's no need to go over, in detail, ground that has already been covered. By way of summary, however, it's useful to build these steps into your planning:

- Unless you're an experienced mentor, get in some 'dress rehearsal' practice before the real event.
- Find out how your role fits into the wider picture by keeping in close contact with your co-teacher educators.
- Ask senior staff for time off timetable for some of your mentoring duties.
- In consultation with your prospective student teachers, arrange a realistic, well-balanced school placement timetable, and incorporate into it opportunities for subject teaching, whole-school issues experience, and tutorials.
- Prior to their arrival, send your student teachers preliminary details about the school; give them copies of the syllabuses they'll be teaching; and provide them either with some appropriate learning resources (notably textbooks) or with information about how to get hold of these items. Assuming most of them will be teaching a National Curriculum subject (as a first and/or a second subject), I also send student teachers a 'National Curriculum made easy' basic information sheet (see Appendix 1).
- Arrange an induction day (or days) for student teachers, and get them acquainted with the institutional culture of the school and with the particular aims and practices of your department.

Liaising

This skill is closely linked to good planning, particularly regarding negotiations

39

and collaborative work with school and university colleagues during the stages referred to in the preceding section. But liaison skills don't start and end with the work leading up to school placements. They continue right through the initial teacher education programme. Here's a checklist of the more important aspects of liaison work that will help you, once placements are up and running:

- The most important liaison work is that which takes place between you and your student teacher. I've come across the expression 'sharp compassion' as a description of the kind of liaison between mentors and intending teachers that should be cultivated. But I'm not happy with the word 'sharp'. I suppose it's intended to convey a sense of not shrinking from 'being cruel to be kind' when this is deemed necessary in the assessment of a student teacher's performance. But I prefer the expression 'honest compassion'.

    I was recently told by a mentor that his student teachers had 'complained' that their tutor was too 'kind', and didn't have the heart to 'tell it like it was' when they thought that they could have done better. In this case, 'honest compassion' might prompt a teacher educator to confirm the student teachers' legitimate concern, and offer some reassuring pointers on how performance might be improved. You won't be helping your student teachers if you're not accurate and candid about what you've observed in their practice.

- Ask other colleagues who are supporting your mentoring work (for example, by providing student teachers with second-subject teaching and form work) to give you brief oral weekly progress reports and short (up to one side of A4) written monthly updates on developing competences.

- Maintain regular contact with tutors (or consortium co-mentors), not just through the official written report channels and respective exchange visits, but also through informal conversations (telephone and/or face-to-face). I sometimes write a letter to a tutor when, for example, commending a student teacher's initiative.

- Stay in touch with other mentors in your school. Too often mentors stay within their own sphere of operation, especially when subject boundaries are involved. It's a good idea, both in terms of institutional coherence and for the healthy exchange of ideas, to meet at least monthly for a brainstorming session with other mentors. Consider too the possibility of meeting up with mentors from other schools in order to widen the pool of expertise.

- Make your services available to student teachers for whom you don't have direct responsibility. Obviously, this has to be done with due courtesy and sensitivity to the responsibilities of other mentors. As a whole-school issues as well as a subject mentor, I probably have more opportunities than most mentors (who tend to be subject mentors only), to extend this invitation in an official capacity.

- Keep the professional tutor, if your school has one, informed about your student teachers' progress. It's also good practice to liaise with the professional tutor (who tends to have a whole-school view of matters) if you write references for student teachers who are seeking first appointments.

Demonstrating

Showing 'how it's done' is an important aspect of good mentoring. In that sense, you're expected, as a mentor, to be an exemplary exponent of your craft. But don't be imperious about this. Having student teachers sitting at the back of the classroom all the time watching the 'maestro' putting on a show won't do much for their confidence. Think about it. How would you feel if you were about to be unleashed upon a class of students who had just seen you formally observing their 'real' teacher? It doesn't do much for the self-esteem, does it? While the 'back of the room' style has its place – offering plenty of scope for uninterrupted watching – I generally prefer student teachers to be observing participants rather than flies on the wall.

Bearing this in mind, here's how I provide student teachers with opportunities to watch me demonstrating my craft:

- Prior to a demonstration lesson, I brief the student teacher on what I'm going to do, I usually suggest some important areas for special focus (e.g. teacher conduct during the opening and closing of a lesson), and I negotiate an important role (e.g. an expert sounding-board for school students to consult during group discussions) for her or him to take on in the ensuing event. It's important that the mentor provides observing student teachers with some background information before the lesson starts. Otherwise, they won't be tuned into the contextual knowledge that you, unlike the observers, have about the underlying factors which impinge upon your classroom practice.

  How, for example, is an uninformed observer going to know, unless she or he is told beforehand, that the reason you rarely praise a particular school student in public is that, when this happens, he gets a lot of 'stick' after the lesson from his 'laddish' mates? There are differing views about whether it's a good idea or not to provide student teachers with structured, 'watch me doing this' observation schedules. Having consulted beginning teachers on this matter, my view echoes their belief that both structured and unstructured observation provide useful learning opportunities. More about this in the next chapter.

- I inform my school students that they'll be gaining from the input of another colleague, a student teacher, who will be supporting me in some future lessons. This is crucially important if I'm to get my school students on the side of the student teacher. They might not all take kindly to an observer in the classroom, and they're more likely to act unnaturally, including sometimes playing up, if they find a passive, note-taking student teacher at the back of the classroom. When they sense that a student teacher has got something to offer as well as to take, they're more likely to treat the 'stranger in their midst' as part of the show, and to act in their usual way.

● I make a special effort to ensure that the demonstration lesson is successful. I know that sounds rather staged, but aren't we all on our best behaviour when we know we're being watched by an inspector, and doesn't our student teacher deserve the same courtesy? So no fumbling around looking for the class register or not having sorted out the cables on the VCR. You've got an audience, so get the preliminaries right. I usually seat the student teacher either in with the school students or close to them at an unoccupied desk. Then I start the lesson with a brief (about ten minutes) whole-class introduction to the theme under consideration. During this preamble, I invite some input ('What do you think about the view that law enforcement in California is very selective, depending on the neighbourhood being policed?') from the student teacher. I often accompany whole-class teaching with group work, and I provide strategic entry points for the student teacher to offer me some support, as well as giving her or him the space to monitor what I'm doing.

● I 'over-demonstrate', particularly during the early period of the student teacher's school placement, key teacher behaviours. Recently, for example, I advised two of my newly arrived interns not to be too desk-bound when they teach. When they came to observe me teaching, I therefore made a special point of moving around the classroom – something I do anyway, but perhaps not quite as energetically as on that occasion. No wonder the tutor of one of my student teachers remarked, after watching her teach, that she was moving around the classroom like a piece of heavy machinery! 'Good for her!', was my reply.

It's also helpful to demonstrate a fairly wide repertoire of class-management and subject-application skills as the lesson gathers pace. That's the best way to make student teachers understand that 'chalk and talk' isn't the only way to relate to a class.

● If I'm able to, I 'think out loud' my actions and their rationale for the benefit of observing student teachers, as I go about my classroom practice. When, for instance, school students are engaged in group work, I sometimes take the opportunity to talk the student teachers through the contextual cues that underpin what I've just done, what I'm doing now, and what I intend to do next: 'Tony deserves approbation for that good answer; I'm giving him a nod and a smile as we speak, and, after the lesson, when I won't embarrass him in front of some of his "laddish" peers, I'll be more effusive with my praise.' By doing this, I'm conveying to student teachers the crucial point that classroom strategies are not 'use anytime tricks of the trade', but rather intelligent skills that require informed selection and application.

- I provide demonstrations in areas of my professional work that lie outside classroom teaching. A simple, effective way to accomplish this is to have student teachers shadowing you: marking and moderating, doing recess, canteen and end-of-school supervisory duties, taking form registers, dealing with routine administrative matters, and attending parents' evenings.

This section has dealt with student teachers watching you demonstrate your professional skills. It's now time to give them a 'piece of the action'.

Facilitating

In his book *Understanding Mentoring* (1995) Peter Tomlinson refers to the process of 'gradual but flexible "scaffolding": that is, support which can be provided but generally removed as the learner becomes independently capable'. I think that's an excellent metaphor for describing the kind of facilitating that effective mentors should provide beginning teachers. We're the coaches, as well as the assessors, of these pre-service practitioners, and it's up to us to calibrate what they are ready for and what they can handle. Facilitating enables student teachers to practise and hone their emerging professional skills within a secure but also a stretching environment. In the mentor survey I carried out, a number of mentors emphasised the importance of providing student teachers with secure, clearly defined, 'bite-size' roles during the early stages.

It's usually best to provide this security by working alongside the student teacher in a co-teacher role for a few weeks, before initiating solo work. But don't be over-prescriptive here. Certain student teachers are confident and competent enough to do some teaching on their own quite early – provided they're comfortable with the class they're working with, and provided they know you're close to hand should assistance be required. For example, I recently mentored two sociology student teachers, both of whom were well qualified in their specialist subject and who were well versed with the A level sociology syllabus that my Year 12 and 13 students follow. The student teachers had watched me teaching these A level students a few times, and they had done some collaborative work with me on these occasions. Before coming to my school (for their main placement), they had each spent about eight days in two different secondary schools over a period of two months, mainly observing but also doing a limited amount of A level sociology teaching.

The student teachers persuaded me to let them 'go it alone' for part of the time, for these reasons:

- prior 'chalk-on-the-hands' experience over the previous two months
- the particular nature of their main teaching brief, namely, working with A level students whom they already knew were unlikely to engage in disruptive behaviour
- my presence as a co-teacher colleague sometimes got in the way of their confidence in themselves to work autonomously.

This readiness (reluctance is probably a more honest description of my feelings at the time!) to part company with those textbook sureties which counsel 'Always walk before running', made me realise that mentoring has just as much, if not more, to do with contexts as it has to do with conventional wisdoms. More importantly, this particular in-context strategy worked well: the interns made excellent progress in solo teaching. That said, the cautious part of me still heeds the more commonly held view among teacher educators that, for most student teachers, a sustained period of successful co-teaching with a mentor should normally precede solo work.

As for marking, student teachers need early and sustained practice at this important professional skill. They mustn't be thrown at unsuspecting exercise books, but should do plenty of moderating with you and other teachers before they take responsibility for assessing the progress of school students.

Observing

In a recently televised dramatisation of life in a tough Liverpool comprehensive school, a mentor points a camcorder the size of a minor planet at a student teacher during a lesson, and says: 'Pretend I'm not here; just carry on as normal'.

If you want to get the best out of your student teachers, don't do that. It's imperative that you make your observing as 'humane' as possible. When you adopt the role of non-participant, 'fly-on-the-wall' observer, inform student teachers that it's perfectly normal for them to feel nervous (I tell them I'm on edge when they watch me!), and that you make allowances for this in your assessment. But don't start off with non-participant observation. It's more considerate – and also very valuable – to begin with participant observation, which means you'll be working alongside student teachers while simultaneously watching what's going on. I'll deal with this, the 'gentler' version, before considering the other type.

Participant observation

Participant observation enables mentors to offer professional support, as well as monitoring the acquisition and development of teaching competences. While it's especially useful during the early stages of initial teacher education – providing a relatively safe environment for the intending practitioner – it's a superb technique to use at any time. Moreover, it doubles as an indispensable strategy for helping student teachers to become effective co-teachers.

In today's schools, co-teaching is becoming an increasingly important professional skill, particularly in the context of vocational (notably GNVQ) and IT courses, where student-centred study and team-style pedagogies are often preferred.

Good co-teaching, allowing for the occasional improvised flourish, is meticulously planned, with each party having clearly defined roles. When I co-teach with my student teachers, I sit down with them beforehand and we produce a script and do a practice run in an empty classroom. Let me illustrate what I mean by referring to a lesson on fair trade between poor and rich countries that I and two social sciences student teachers gave to a class of Year 12 students. We decided to make the lesson a real 'hands-on', taste-buds-stimulating event, by bringing in fairly traded food, coffee and tea for the school students to sample. Our respective roles in the forthcoming lesson were rehearsed beforehand without an audience.

During the actual event, I served the coffee (in mugs with the 'cafedirect' logo, a fair-trade product mark), one of the student teachers served tea, and the other passed round chocolate bars and candied raisins. After the school students (and, of course, I and the student teachers) had finished this very tasty snack, the student teachers introduced the next part of the lesson.

They gave a short talk on the work and aims of the fair trade companies whose products had just been consumed. They linked the aims of fair trade to the Global Civic Ethic promoted by the Report of the Commission on Global Governance, *Our Global Neighbourhood* (1995), which endorses the rights of all human beings 'to an opportunity to earn a fair living and provide for their own welfare'.

In that context, and germane to the syllabus they're following, the school students were divided into three groups for 15 minutes and asked to respond to this question: Should social science get involved in the promotion of social justice or should it honestly and objectively report facts, or should it do both these things? Given that the preceding event was clearly designed to elicit the first or third of these alternatives, you might reasonably argue that this was a leading question. That said, I positively encourage my school students not to adopt the face-value view that teacher always knows best – they're used to being 'critical' when they weigh up arguments.

45

But, on this occasion, my student teachers and I endeavoured to submit our case that sociology should be both objective and emancipatory. We were very explicit about this, so the school students were left in no doubt as to the 'one-sided' polemic we were presenting. Sometimes it's right to argue a case forcefully and passionately. I'm reminded here of Jonathan Kozol's (1993) concern about the 'undevoted apathy of mediocre class discussion' and about the need for school students 'to speak with full irreverence, but without the terror of retaliation'.

After the groups reported back their deliberations, I asked the class to make a display chart out of the wrappers and boxes in which the food and drink had been packed. Not only was the packaging very striking, it also contained information on how and where the various items had been produced and traded in markets that gave workers in poor countries a fair price for their labour. After 30 minutes the display was complete, and very impressive it is too, adding visual appeal and shared conviction to our classroom.

While I believe the lesson was a success, one of the difficulties associated with participant observation like this is how to record accurately the observed event. Ideally, this would be done during the observation. Sometimes, jottings can be made when your 'co-teacher student' is taking the lead, and such quickly snatched notes can later trigger accurate recall and reconstruction of what was observed. In practice, however, opportunities to observe, participate and record simultaneously are often limited – unless you've got a camera-operated surveillance system! So the next best thing is to do what I did after the lesson described above: make notes as soon as possible. Recall is quite sharp then, but it diminishes rapidly thereafter.

Non-participant observation

Clinical it is, but this kind of 'fly on the wall' observation, whereby the mentor watches without participating, is vital in order to give student teachers more space to do their own thing and to monitor what's happening in a non-interventionist way. The non-interventionist aspect is crucial. Unless your assistance is asked for by the student teacher or unless a crisis develops that she or he clearly can't handle alone, it's best to remain strictly on the sidelines. Nothing is more disconcerting to an intern than to have you stealing the show when it's not your turn to do so. With this in mind, when you're a non-participant observer, it's important to avoid these intrusions:

- asking the student teacher if you can address the whole class for a few moments before handing over to her/him
- offering unsolicited contributions when the student teacher is in the driving seat

- engaging in private asides with school students ('Why haven't you handed in that assignment yet Sarah?') while the lesson is in progress.

On the other hand, these are definite 'DO's':

Brief the student teacher beforehand on:

- What's to be observed. It's usually best to indicate a focus or focuses. As a general rule, I focus on these areas: subject knowledge, subject application, and class management.
- How the observation is to be monitored. I use a self-designed lesson observation schedule (see Figure 1, p. 48) which doubles as a continuous assessment for the student teacher to retain in a rolling portfolio. The student teacher keeps the original (a deserved courtesy); I keep the copy.
- A negotiated contingency plan which permits me to intervene if a very awkward incident arises that's beyond what a beginning teacher might reasonably be expected to handle (e.g. 'heavy duty' disruptive behaviour on the part of a member of the class).
- When feedback (oral and written) is to be provided. There's a simple principle here: 'the sooner, the fresher, the better'.

Generally, it's best to watch entire rather than part lessons as a non-participant observer. Otherwise, you won't get a feel for the whole event and might, as I've sometimes done, advise the student teacher to employ a strategy that she or he was going to use before you exited the classroom. I know, of course, that not all mentors will have the time to act on this advice. However, if you just observe part of a lesson, it's not very helpful to watch less than half an hour of the action, unless you're focusing on a particular issue (e.g. how a student teacher settles a class during the first few minutes).

Assessing

If you teach a National Curriculum subject, you've probably spent lots of evenings ploughing through 'bite-size' chunks of knowledge called 'statements of attainment', ticking them off as the students accomplish them. But the days of tick-list assessment are over. Statements of attainment have been replaced by 'level descriptions', which provide a more rounded judgement of overall student performance at the end of each key stage.

Gerald Haigh (1995) eloquently likens the reform of National Curriculum assessment procedures to the difference between measuring the temperature of a hot metal ingot with a pyrometer (the equivalent of statements of attainment ticks), and getting an experienced steelworker to spit on the metal, listen to the

Assessment of DFEE Professional Competences re subject knowledge, subject application and class management

Department: Year/Level/Subject/Topic: /   /   /

Date: Time: Student teacher:

1)   Subject knowledge

This is good   Consider this advice

2) Subject application

This is good   Consider this advice

3) Class management

This is good   Consider this advice

Comments from student teacher (particularly goal-setting). Continue over if necessary.

Mentor/Supervising teacher:

Figure 1 Lesson observation schedule

sizzle, and announce the temperature to the nearest 10 degrees Celsius (the equivalent of level description judgements).

If the measurement of students' learning could be calibrated with the accuracy of a sophisticated thermometer, teachers would probably be happy to stick with a rigid tick-list system. But this isn't the case: getting a meaningful fix on the fantastic achievements of the human brain sometimes requires a 'best-fit' calculation. This isn't a question of razor-sharp precision versus vaguely felt hunch; it's more a matter of recognising that something as complex as educational attainment needs an ample appraisal rather than a cursory tick.

Regular assessment and constructive feedback, both spoken and written, are essential if student teachers are to know what they're doing well (always find something to praise first – unless, as is unlikely, everything is a disaster!), and how they need to improve and extend their professional skills. It's especially helpful to give an assessment of performance and some guidance on future strategies as soon as possible after observing a student teacher in action. In my experience, student teachers appreciate this courtesy immensely: it satisfies that 'How did I do?' sense of urgency that all performers seem to possess, and it has an immediacy that student teachers can make sense of and relate to.

Assessment procedures vary between subjects and levels, but the most important task of the mentor is to help student teachers, as appropriate, to:

- Take account of National Curriculum and public examination criteria, and accurately incorporate them into their formative (each piece of work at a time) and summative (end of: course, key stage, year, etc.) assessment.
- Use assessment diagnostically, namely by setting realistic learning targets based on the prior attainments of individual school students.
- Employ subject- and department-specific, as well as whole-school, marking procedures. In my department, for example, I encourage the use of green ink (a traditional editor style) when marking. The school also has a cross-curriculum procedure for correcting punctuation and spelling errors.
- Mark attainment outcomes objectively: otherwise, school students won't know what's expected of them in important tests like public examinations. But recognise and reward genuine effort, whatever the level of attainment, with supportive comments.

As indicated above, you need to provide both spoken and written assessment to student teachers.

Spoken assessment

This kind of assessment is most usually offered after the mentor has observed the student teacher teaching. It's best given in the form of a diagnostic summary of what's going well and needs to be continued, and what might be done to enhance teaching skills in certain areas. You should reassure the student teacher that the highlighting of performance improvement strategies is not a negative, fault-finding exercise. On the contrary, it's an integral part of professional development, and occurs in both pre- and in-service appraisal.

When I give advice on target setting, I make a distinction between actions I've observed that are best not continued (e.g. unrealistic admonitions, like insisting on absolute silence when peer communication is appropriate), and things I haven't seen that should be tried out in future (e.g. the suggestion to actively involve more school students in lessons).

I also provide spoken assessment when I talk to my student teachers about their progress in the marking of school students' work. This generally occurs in the form of 'comparing notes' after we've both marked the same work. In terms of scores, if student teachers have clearly over- or under-marked (quite usual, especially at the beginning of the school placement), I tell them this and explain where they went wrong. If they have got it about right, we negotiate the final score, and I adjust my marks if they convince me that their judgement is better. If they've given a score that exactly matches the one I've awarded, I warmly congratulate them.

We talk too about the kind of comments made on pieces of work, and other matters germane to the marking style.

Written assessment

For this, I generally use the lesson observation schedule referred to earlier (Figure 1, p. 48), which provides written assessments of performance in relation to the DfEE competences most readily displayed in classroom teaching: subject knowledge; subject application; and class management. I usually report on how student teachers are progressing in assessing the work of the school students they teach in the university pro formas referred to below.

You'll note that the lesson observation schedule is divided into two vertical columns: 'This is good' (i.e. keep it up!) and 'Consider this advice' (which contains target-setting guidance). Previously, I used the designations 'strengths' and 'limitations', but I think that 'limitations' is unnecessarily negative. Is it appropriate to describe real progress in a competence where improvement is still needed as a limitation? I don't think so. Moreover, the admonition to 'Consider this advice' reinforces the crucial message that target-setting is normal and essential in all aspects of professional development.

My lesson observation schedules for main-placement student teachers are accompanied by these written reports (with the exception of the first item, all are university pro formas; all reports are sent to university tutors, and copied to student teachers):

- a settling-in letter (two weeks into the main placement)
- a tick-box, 'Your progress has been satisfactory ...', 'Your progress indicates a need for improvement in the areas indicated ...', 'Your progress causes us to be concerned ...' report (a month into the main placement)
- two progress reports
- a final summative report towards the end of the main placement.

Samples of these reports – filled in, but with real names changed, to protect confidentiality – are provided in Appendix 2. As mentioned earlier, I also send informal letters to the university to commend student teachers for special initiatives and particular successes, as and when appropriate. Like all forms of written assessment, the student teachers receive copies of these letters.

Openness here is just and necessary. The worst excesses of 'boss management' abuse escape unnoticed and unchallenged when those in power make disparaging and unfounded allegations about interns (and even other colleagues) in so-called 'confidential' progress reports and references. Thankfully, in these more enlightened days of 'freedom of information', student and qualified teachers' rights of access to such references, as long as they're contained on electronic files, are safeguarded under the 1984 Data Protection Act.

Not everything, however, should be measured against the criteria laid down by 'invisible experts' in Westminster, and translated into things called DfEE competences. Hazel Hagger et al. (1993) describe how mentors can help student teachers to become adept at self-assessment by providing what is termed 'partnership supervision'. This refers to the process whereby your post-lesson debriefing 'consists of the data collected during your observation, which you explain if necessary, but do not evaluate'. The onus here is on giving objective, non-judgemental feedback.

Instead of, for example, saying 'You should have involved more of the class in the discussion', the mentor might note 'You involved about two-thirds of the class in the discussion'. While this might appear leading, the idea is to encourage the student teacher to give an explanation of what the mentor has observed. There might be a good reason why the remaining third of the class weren't invited to join a particular discussion: perhaps they had been primed beforehand to listen rather than speak for this part of the lesson. On the other hand, the student teacher may have 'forgotten' to engage certain members of the class in what should have been a whole-class encounter. Either way, the student teacher's motives are not pre-empted by the mentor. Rather, the student teacher is invited to reflect upon, explain and evaluate what she or he has done.

All teachers, whether involving pre- or in-service professional development, need to be able to evaluate their own performance. Getting them to talk through the reasoning behind their actions promotes this important process. So, too, does the practice of asking them to consider what kind of teachers they are/want to be, and the extent to which they believe they've achieved this goal.

I, for example, want to be the kind of teacher who makes low-achieving school students feel that things might and can be otherwise, that there's still time and a way to turn things around and leave school with a future to look forward to. I judge my own performance in this context by the number of such school students whom I help to get successfully through a post-16 course (not always with a high pass score, I concede), and who then enter higher education or secure a career-ladder job (more often than not after I've 'plea-bargained' with a university admissions tutor or an employer).

Some educationists suggest that self-assessment should be preceded by mentor assessment. I don't agree. I think both types of assessment should be conducted simultaneously. Student teachers need a subjective awareness of how things are developing, as well as objective feedback from a mentor.

Guiding

Here are, in my view, the three most important types of guidance that underpin effective mentoring:

- skills guidance
- ethical guidance
- counselling guidance.

Skills guidance

The 'walk before run' principle is a useful reminder that the professional competences which we now tend to take for granted in our own teaching didn't just land on our laps overnight. It's therefore vital that we open up our own practice quite explicitly to those whom we mentor. Ideally, this might involve an '*in situ* running commentary', with student teachers watching and listening as we conduct our lessons – a bit like those television series pathologists who talk into a microphone as they go about their business!

There are, of course, only limited possibilities (which should be seized upon) for this kind of learning model in mentoring. Unless your school students are busy working and don't require close supervision, it's very difficult to teach and to talk about your teaching simultaneously. But you should give interns an immediate post-lesson debriefing on your own practice whenever possible. This might involve, for example, a once-weekly 15-minute slot when a lesson is straightaway followed by a recess or the end of the school day. They'll gain a much fuller understanding of what they've just watched if you accompany at least some of your lessons with follow-up discussions.

As far as your observation of student teachers is concerned, this should be followed with:

- Affirmative support and encouragement, with some fine-tuning guidance if appropriate, when things have gone well (e.g. 'It's right that you didn't humiliate that late-arriving student in public when he entered the classroom, but it's a good idea to have a quiet word with him about what he needs to do if this happens again.').
- Fairly directive guidance when actions haven't elicited desirable outcomes, and where health and safety procedures haven't been followed (e.g. 'To maximise whole-class participation, don't just direct questions to students who have their hands up'; 'Ensure that all the class wear protective goggles during these experiments.').
- The posing of alternative strategies when there appears to be a need for a more effective way forward (e.g. 'Instead of pointing at students in an unfamiliar class during question and answer sessions, why not consider calling out students by name, using the class register?').
- Promoting, particularly, as student teachers become more confident, their habits of self-reflection and self-appraisal. While they rightly look to you for practical instruction, they also need to find their feet and develop their own distinctive styles.

As far as their assessment of the progress of school students is concerned, your guidance to student teachers should emphasise that supportive feedback is as important as 'clinical' objectivity.

Ethical guidance

I recently received a letter from an American professor of education, in which he wrote:

> the case for principled practice ... is compelling. It's funny, but I've discovered over the years that it isn't as hard a case to make as is often assumed – who, after all, would argue for unprincipled practice, at least who would do so who cares at all about educating the young?

It's perhaps harder, though, to define what's meant by 'principled practice' than it is to agree with the good professor's argument. This point has been amply considered in the previous chapter, so it makes little sense to re-examine it again at length. Suffice it to say, by way of summary, that I believe principled practice is characterised by the conscientious efforts of a teacher to:

- bring out the best, in terms of learning achievements, credentialised and otherwise, of her or his school students
- demonstrably care about the psychological, physical and social well-being of her or his school students
- encourage, by example and through teaching, her or his school students to strive for social justice, and to repudiate racism, sexism and all destructive '-isms'.

For me, the above goals seem self-evidently principled, but your view of 'principled' might not necessarily coincide with mine. Here we encounter a profound philosophical dilemma: is there an absolute definition of 'principled'? You might remember from the previous chapter that if there is, I don't claim to know or to have privileged access to this definition. That said, for the purposes of going about my professional work, I define my felt beliefs as explicitly as possible, and then seek to act on them, whether or not they coincide with a particular institutional culture. If your convictions and mine don't coincide, we're at least acting on our principles when we practise what we believe in.

I think that, as mentors, we should tell our student teachers what ethical considerations guide our professional work, but we can't force our morality upon those who might have radically different opinions. I haven't yet come across a student teacher who has challenged the beliefs that inform my own practice. I can't be certain that this is due to their not wanting to upset me, but I don't think this is so. I've always sought to cultivate an atmosphere of open dialogue in my dealings with student teachers, and I think they feel comfortable about voicing their genuine views, rather than saying what they think I might want to hear. But even if I'm wrong about this assumption, the main thing is that the consideration of ethical issues features prominently in the guidance I offer student teachers. This means that, irrespective of how we might define the concept of 'principled', I want initial teacher education to foster an awareness of moral purpose and, above all, a readiness to care for school students.

Let me illustrate the last point with an example of some ethical guidance I gave one of my student teachers during the spring term of 1995. It transpired during one of our discussions that one of my school students had left the premises, seemingly with my signed permission. However, the signature on the exit slip which he left at the school reception looked like a forgery, and a colleague in charge of attendance monitoring came to check if the exit slip bore my real signature.

It didn't. I called the school student at home, and asked him directly if he'd forged my signature. He wouldn't admit that he had, but I didn't want to embarrass him by forcing a confession, so I asked him to follow correct procedure in future, and left it at that. I subsequently reported what action I'd taken to the student teacher, explaining that I knew this student was encountering severe difficulties at home which might have accounted for his out-of-character action, and what he needed more than anything else was a sympathetic hearing rather than a 'You're on report if this happens against' threat.

Following on from this, I advised the student teacher to regard the matter as an example of how important it is to look beyond a school student's behaviour that, on the surface, might appear to warrant a stern admonition, yet, on deeper examination, is found to be symptomatic of an underlying problem. I hope this guidance will encourage my student teacher not to invoke sanctions automatically when a seemingly inappropriate behaviour has occurred, especially when that behaviour is uncharacteristic of the school student concerned. After all, teaching isn't just a technical exercise; it's an ethical activity, and 'bareknuckled' styles are inappropriate.

Counselling

A mentor colleague, an English teacher, told me recently that one of his student teachers was very upset when a whole-class discussion she had meticulously planned for a Year 10 class went disastrously wrong. The school students were plainly uninterested in her efforts to engage them in debate, and they remained irritatingly silent for much of the time. Not taking the hint and changing tack, she made matters worse by resolutely sticking to her original lesson plan. Before long, some school students started playing up, and things rapidly turned from bad to worse. I hear you saying 'Been there', 'Seen it', 'Done it', which is what my mentor colleague said, in an attempt to rally his spirit-broken student teacher. But he knew that his readiness to empathise with her was only the start of a counselling process that also required some supportive guidance. In this situation, and in similar situations when pre-planned lessons don't go as planned, what's needed is a strategy that provides a realistic way forward should the problem arise again. In the example just referred to, the main thing is to ensure that contingency procedures are built into the planning. Thus, if a whole-class discussion doesn't take off, it's probably a good idea to switch to some task-oriented group work, returning perhaps to the wider audience by getting groups to report back their deliberations, in turn, to the rest of the class.

More often than not, as a mentor, your counselling skills will be needed in situations, like the one described above, that are linked to difficulties experienced by the student teacher with subject-application and class-management skills. In that context, loss of face is a recurrent theme. To help restore your student teacher's confidence, you should:

- be very approachable; if that's not a part of your usual style, work hard at cultivating this quality
- demonstrate empathy: 'I've experienced the same kind of difficulties myself' often works wonders
- map out of a better action plan for future reference when a student teacher is having problems
- avoid creating an artificially contrived 'crisis' in order to try out the agreed strategy; let nature take its course here, and be generous by way of approbation when, as it surely will, your wise counsel yields the right results.

Of course, counselling isn't only a form of 'psychological first-aid' to be summoned when a crisis looms. Effective mentors can enhance the 'feel-good' factor of student teachers by:

- Becoming acquainted with their personalities and with their interests beyond the classroom, thereby relating to them on an individual as well as on a professional level.
- Creating real 'quality-time' slots for them to come for a chat about anything that's on their minds, rather than making them feel that their concerns are getting in the way of your busy schedule. I tell my student teachers that I'm available for consultation during any recess. There are few takers, but they know the offer is genuine.
- Cultivating an accepting stance towards them for who they are as human beings rather than seeking to mould them into 'Do as I say' functionaries; yet, at the same time, introducing an element of gentle directiveness by pointing them in the right way.
- Advising them that a certain amount of stress, especially in the early stages of getting to know a class, is normal, and is likely to diminish as people get to know each other.

Ultimately, the measure of your effectiveness as a counselling mentor will be the extent to which you're able to help student teachers develop their own strategies for dealing with both the unpredictable and the routine aspects of professional practice. The knack is to strike the right balance between being overly protective and unduly remote. There's no hard and fast rule here because different student teachers have different personalities, different confidence levels and different needs. Nevertheless, it's no bad thing to let all your student teachers know that you're an approachable, congenial type, and that your goal isn't to undermine their confidence but to help them realise their true potential.

Having unpacked and identified the generic skills required by effective mentors, it's now time to suggest practical ways of putting those skills to good use by helping student teachers to become 'competent' exponents of their craft. Chapters 5–7 will consequently offer guidance on how to employ the skills of planning, liaising, demonstrating, facilitating, observing, assessing and guiding, as those skills apply to the mentoring of these competences:

- subject knowledge, teaching strategies and class management
- assessing school students
- whole-school issues.

GUIDANCE POINTS _____

1 Mentoring involves generic skills, notably: planning, liaising, demonstrating, facilitating, observing, assessing, and guiding. These skills are not discrete; they overlap.

2 Mentors should be involved in all stages of the planning of initial teacher education programmes.

3 Prior to beginning their first mentoring duties, mentors-elect should get in some 'dry-run' practice under the supervision of an experienced mentor or a professional tutor.

4 Mentors need to negotiate realistic timetabling provision in order to do their important work. Don't forget that most secondary school student teachers spend at least two-thirds of a one-year course with mentor teacher educators.

5 Before they arrive, student teachers should be sent details of the school and the department(s) concerned.

6 Mentors, in co-operation with student teachers, university tutors and other supervising teachers, should furnish student teachers with a timetable that provides: first- and second-subject teaching; experience of whole-school issues; weekly reflective seminars; and a reasonable amount of non-contact time.

7 Prior to the start of school placements, mentors should provide student teachers with one or two on-site induction days.

8 When opening their professional practice to intending teachers, mentors should let the interns observe as participants and as non-participants, and they should exemplify excellence in what they demonstrate.

9 The over-demonstration of effective teacher behaviours (e.g. starting a lesson) is greatly appreciated by student teachers, particularly in the early stages.

10   Student teachers need to observe and work with different teachers (not just in classrooms) who are able to demonstrate varying approaches and techniques.

11   Facilitating is usually best initiated by giving student teachers 'bite-size', achievable but stretching tasks, in a fairly structured learning environment. As confidence increases, 'bite-size' should become 'bigger chunks', graduating to 'whole tasks'.

12   Assessment needs to be accurate but supportive, and it should generate realistic target-setting. Spoken and written assessments are needed; both should be provided sooner rather than later. Mentors need to realise that they're assessing beginning competences, that is, the potential to become an effective teacher rather than a finished product.

13   Student teachers should be encouraged to assess their own performance, right from day one.

14   When mentors provide guidance, they should: be as explicit as possible in making their own best practice available for the observation and scrutiny of student teachers; present a compelling case for principled practice; and provide counselling that embraces a concern for student teachers as human beings rather than as a form of crisis-driven 'psychological first aid'.

CHAPTER 5

Subject knowledge, teaching strategies and class management

Effective teachers know their subject and teach it skilfully by creating and managing a positive behavioural and learning environment. Effective mentors help student teachers to become effective teachers. The achievement of that goal, as far as DfEE criteria on subject knowledge, teaching strategies and class management are concerned, requires mentors to help equip new entrants to the profession with the accredited competence to:

- demonstrate secure subject knowledge, and teach to the school curriculum

(notably in the context of the National Curriculum and public examinations)

- plan and teach coherent lessons
- set realistic learning tasks
- employ relevant, stimulating teaching strategies and resources (including IT)
- use clear language and promote school students' language and communication skills
- develop and maintain an orderly classroom atmosphere
- employ whole-class, group, pair, and individual teaching strategies, as appropriate.

It's your job, as a mentor, to furnish relevant opportunities, accurate assessment and supportive guidance for student teachers to gain and fulfil these competences. The advice that follows will help you accomplish these important goals.

Planning

Providing student teachers with opportunities to learn and practise professional skills in classroom settings requires careful initial planning. Moreover, given that your prototype designs have to be trialled in classrooms, the results will sometimes lead to revised follow-up planning (in consultation with your student teachers) for future lessons. That said, it's important to draw up an original plan (consult student teachers here, but encourage them to take brief notes on your suggested 'have a go' strategies) that's likely to yield positive outcomes.

The way I do this is by briefing my student teachers on:

- What kind of subject knowledge (if any) the school students already possess, and an approximate indication of what level they're at in terms of ability (are they predominantly 'high', 'average' or 'below average' achievers, or is there a wide attainment range?). With few exceptions, I find student teachers overestimate the abilities of the classes they're going to teach. It's therefore very important that mentors give thorough advice on the setting of realistic learning tasks and on the use of clear language and understandable terminology. Are most Key Stage 4 history students in a particular class, for example, likely to know the meaning of words like 'monastic', 'puritan' and 'papal' without explanation?

- The curriculum knowledge and skills (including IT) that must be taught when school students are following a particular course. Do emphasise that adherence to National Curriculum and public examination syllabuses is essential. Otherwise, coherence in terms of planning and teaching within and between classes can easily stray from the track into diversions that might be fascinating, but that won't necessarily help school students pass tests and examinations. If they get the lesson planning right here, student teachers are more likely to teach to the prescribed curriculum and to remain within a coherent framework that school students can relate to and make sense of.

As far as actual lesson plans are concerned, things have changed since I did my teaching practice in an East London comprehensive school some twenty years ago. Then, teaching practice supervisors expected student teachers to produce copious lesson plans, running to several pages in length. Nowadays, a standardised A4 sheet provided by the university is the usual format. It's concise, focused and punchy. Please refer to Appendix 3 for a sample. One of the things I particularly look for is the inclusion of appropriate and stimulating resources in the planning. Student teachers often bring a freshness and a vitality to this task. I always go through lesson plans with student teachers prior to observing them putting the plans into action.

- The kind of 'orderliness' that's most likely to work in the particular classes they're teaching. When they're working with Year 12 and Year 13 maths students, for example, they don't need to be as openly directive in constructing and sustaining an orderly atmosphere as they might have to be in a classroom of 30 or more Year 7 geographers. But in neither situation do they need to impose an expedient silence or a repressive conformity. For me, 'orderliness' means that I can conduct my lesson without the distracting intrusions of disruptive behaviour – aggressive or otherwise – on the part of my students. This goal can be achieved through humane means.

- The institutional cues that form the taken-for-granted code of conduct of most students in the school, referring to the rules contained in school prospectuses and other official documents, and outlining the general expectations of most of the teachers. I advise the student teachers to behave in a manner which generally supports this script. A former student teacher friend of mine, on the first day of his teaching practice in a comprehensive school where the dominant control culture was of the 'make my day enforcer' type, told students to 'Call me Mike'. Thereafter, Mike's students gave him a very hard time indeed! Student teachers need to know that an awareness of what routine procedures prevail in a particular school is a powerful aid to effective class management. For their part, school students seem unfailingly knowledgeable in such matters, and they don't always take kindly to indecisiveness on the part of teachers. I hasten to add that 'Ms or Mr Don't mess with me' is, thankfully, not the persona adopted by most teachers these days.

Finally, during this part of the briefing, I make certain that student teachers know and don't break school rules, and don't act illegally. Clearly, matters like notification to parents in the event of after-school detentions, and the admonition never to use physical punishment, are crucially important in these areas.

- The need to strike a realistic balance between practising their felt convictions and not rocking the institutional boat in a manner that creates procedural confusion. If this sounds like pragmatism, it's not the kind of pragmatism that puts a brutal option before an ethical approach, but one that finds achievable opportunities to act out one's authentic humanity. Even so, I tell my student teachers that when I'm called to do a last-lesson substitution with a tough class whom I don't normally teach, I tend to stick broadly within the institutional culture – if it helps my 'survival'!

- The teaching styles and class-management techniques that seem to promote learning gains and co-operative behaviour in students. No doubt, like me, much of this will be based on your own experiences and tried and tested routines. That's fine, but it's important not to be too parochial here. So do share, in discussions with your student teachers, the insights and practices of other colleagues: from 'chalk and talk' exponents to 'student-centred learning' advocates, from 'easy-going coaxers' to 'strict disciplinarians'. It's not for me to tell you, an experienced teacher, what approaches are best. We know, from the work we do, that the art of teaching is too complex to come up with universal principles, even though our student teachers are sometimes, understandably, looking for 'quick-fix recipe knowledge'.

With that caveat in mind, this is the advice I offer my student teachers. I suggest that they seek to become:

a) adept at mixing and matching teaching styles to appropriate learning needs, but not too much inclined towards methods that involve excessive dictation and lengthy lectures

b) 'indulgent persuaders' who seek to create and sustain an enjoyment of learning, rather than 'boss managers' who believe in 'no pain, no gain'.

In support of this counsel, I inform them that motivation, as well as positive behaviour and learning, are more contingent on harnessing interest and providing achievable but stretching learning tasks, than on engendering irksome vacillation and inappropriately pitched expectations. Lest student teachers doubt this – and why should they take my word for it? – I refer them to appropriate published evidence: the Elton Report (DES, 1989) is especially apposite.

After the first planning stage, I check – and if necessary, suggest amendments to – my student teachers' lesson plans. Then I let them try their hand, and they report back on this 'experimentation' during our once-weekly seminars or, if they prefer, at any other time. The feedback here confirms that what they're doing:

- is working well and should generally be continued
- is working well in some respects but is unhelpful in other contexts, and needs to be modified
- isn't working at all well and requires a different approach.

It's important to realise, however, that if modifications or changes seem necessary, this doesn't usually mean that the pre-lesson plans aren't good ones. It's more likely to indicate that further observation of experienced teachers working to the same script is required, to be followed, perhaps, with some 'imitative' practice. In that sense, post-lesson planning shouldn't often require radical reshaping of the original idea.

Liaising

It's always helpful to make sure that student teachers get to watch other teachers managing classes, not just in classrooms, gyms and sportsfields, but in corridors, canteens and bus-bays. After all, you don't want them to become mentor clones! If you have a professional tutor in your school, ask her or him to liaise with these colleagues in order to set up meaningful observation (and, whenever feasible, some supervised practice). Like me, you'll also need to do a bit of 'beg, steal and borrow'. The problem is that one is tempted to approach only those colleagues whom one judges are likely to offer assistance (that's why a professional tutor comes in very handy), but do look further afield. As indicated previously, try to ensure that your liaising work provides a good range of role models.

Effective liaison on your part should ensure that these opportunities are made available to intending teachers:

- Watching and, whenever possible, supporting teachers of different subjects in the classroom, and talking to them afterwards. Two or three, including the head of special needs, would be excellent. Make sure that the observation of teachers and school students using IT is featured in the watching brief.
- Shadowing and assisting form tutors during registrations and 'active tutorial work' (e.g. whole-form projects on road safety).
- Consulting colleagues who have important curriculum and pastoral responsibilities (notably heads of department and heads of year) about teaching styles and class-management strategies. I don't expect these busy teachers to

offer appointments (but if they do, fine): an informal chat over a cup of tea in the staffroom is what I usually ask for – and I haven't been turned down yet!

As far as liaison with teacher educator colleagues is concerned, much of this is likely to be accomplished through official written reports, copied to the student teachers, on progress in the designated competences. I usually let student teachers decide whether or not to show their lesson observation reports to the professional tutor and university tutors. I think it's important that you give them 'ownership' of these documents, which, after all, are principally designed to help them deal with the practicalities of classroom teaching.

Your liaison with student teachers will (or should!) occur on a daily basis. Most of it will be on a spoken level, with written documentation provided as appropriate. Try to cultivate a friendly, supportive but professional rapport with student teachers, and accord them the same respect you give qualified teachers.

I do a lot of informal liaising with student teachers in the staffroom. It's crucial that mentors make them feel fully entitled to sit and chat with you and other colleagues here. The professional tutor in my school seeks to ensure that all staff make intending teachers very welcome in the staffroom. She also gets mentors to introduce student teachers to the various 'sub-cultural networks' (often but not exclusively subject-based) that occupy different seating areas. Otherwise, there's a real likelihood that interns will all sit together.

To engender even more sociability on the liaison front, I invite my student teachers to a departmental dinner in town with my colleagues and me as hosts, at least once during the main school placement.

Demonstrating

During an informal interview that a science mentor and I conducted with about fifteen PGCE student teachers towards the end of their course, one of the science specialists said he found rather structured, 'going through the motions' demonstrations by my colleague helpful in terms of getting a feel for how to seat and settle Key Stage 3 science classes. There's a subject culture at work here. Science teachers place a high premium on procedural regularities in learning areas where unpredictable behaviour could easily lead to accidents.

It was therefore interesting (and impressive) to find, in the mentor survey I conducted, that a science mentor at another school set aside a whole day for showing student teachers how to practise and promote 'safety in science'. I often hear science student teachers at my school remarking how useful they find it to watch technicians setting up equipment prior to lessons. That's another avenue you might usefully explore if you want your student teachers (and not just the scientists) to see clearly defined, sequential practice accomplished by experts. Performing and visual arts, craft, design and technology, and sports and PE also offer useful opportunities for student teachers to watch highly systemised modes of class management.

This regimented kind of orderliness doesn't mean that lessons containing substantial practical activities are purveyed by exponents of the 'I'm the boss and you better believe it' school of class management. When activities concerning the health and safety of students are in the frame, as for example in science laboratories and gym halls, all teachers must be confidently directive. This isn't to suggest that assuredness in taking the lead on supervisory matters is only found among teachers of practical subjects. It's a generic skill that crosses subject boundaries, and while it conveys a teacher's capacity to take charge in a class management sense, it has nothing to do with being progressive or traditional.

It's also important that your student teachers don't just watch colleagues who never seem to put a foot wrong in the way they manage classes. It's not that I purposely stage a mishap, or, worse still, arrange for my student teachers to watch a colleague who just can't cope in front of a difficult class. Both options are unethical. At the same time, given that most of us mentors don't always get it right in the work that we do, it's salutary that student teachers should be given the chance to learn from our mistakes, as well as from our better moments. They also need to know – from the 'by proxy' experience of being there when we slip up – that we, as mentors, feel for them when they encounter setbacks.

Creating opportunities

But what kind of 'being there' do I arrange for my student teachers, when I get them to observe me and other colleagues who are teaching and managing classes? In the early stages of their school-based programme, I usually follow (and politely ask my colleagues to follow) this procedure:

- In general, brief the student teachers on key aspects of teaching styles and class-management tactics that they need to monitor, notably how we open and close lessons, how we relate to school students, how we use whole-class and group methods, and what happens when we respond to any 'critical incidents' that might arise. In particular, 'up-front', directive supervisory skills, like taking a register or settling a class at the start of a lesson, are more helpfully demonstrated and observed in a fairly structured way. Technical operations, for instance, using a CD-ROM or an OHP, also tend to require a focused approach.

  Do include, however, some opportunities for beginning teachers to observe lessons that haven't been signposted in advance, as far as 'things to watch out for' are concerned. This 'let it happen' way of looking at experienced teachers is appreciated by student teachers for its natural, uncontrived qualities. In his now classic study of a 1930s Boston gang, the sociologist William Foote Whyte (1943) illustrated how important it is not to pre-empt social inquiry too much when he wrote: 'As I sat and listened, I learned the answers to questions that I would not even have had the sense to ask if I had been getting my information solely on an interviewing basis'.

If I may evoke a parallel, sometimes your student teachers will learn the answers to questions they hadn't thought about, if they're given the chance to tune into those aspects of your teaching that haven't been pre-arranged and scripted for viewing.

- Arrange for the student teachers to be exclusively or primarily non-participant, note-taking observers before they become co-teaching observers. Sometimes, especially at the university, this can be introduced through the screening of videos. But there's nothing quite like the real thing. In the partnership scheme to which I belong, student teachers spend much of their first three months of the one-year PGCE course engaging in this kind of observation, starting with two weeks in a primary school.

  While I have some misgivings (stated earlier in the book) about having student teachers merely watching and noting rather than watching and doing, it's important, especially in the early stage of the course, that they get the chance to concentrate closely on recording what they see. I have to concede that non-participant observation is probably the best way of doing this. However, don't feel that this has to be a binding rule. If, during non-participant observation, a genuine opportunity arises to bring the student teacher into the action, then, with her or his consent, do so.

- During about the fourth month of the school-based programme (which, in the course I work on, constitutes the main placement), move more into an 'apprenticeship' model of observation, whereby the teacher demonstrates and the student teacher engages in some imitative (and, of course, as confidence builds, some innovative) practice. There's still a place for some non-participant observation, though, but negotiate how much is needed with the student teachers themselves. Remember too that this type of observation might more readily be adopted when your student teachers watch other teachers.

- Provide plenty of opportunities for student teachers to watch expert demonstrations of IT skills. For practical reasons, I usually do this during recess, demonstrating basic but important computer competences, like creating a document, simple keyboard and mouse skills, and formatting, searching, saving, opening and printing a document. Clearly, this needs to be accompanied with 'have a go' practice.

  More about that in the next section.

Facilitating

In lessons, the facilitation of class-teaching and class-management competences is best initiated in a co-teaching environment. Good learning and co-operative behaviour are ultimately dependent on the ability to build positive relationships with school students. An effective way to help student teachers to do this is to:

- set up some group work (four school students per group if possible)
- arrange for the student teacher to spend up to about five minutes if possible with each group in a clearly defined helping role.

As well as being a gentle icebreaker, this simple technique gives all the students in the class the chance to get acquainted with the student teacher on an inter-personal level. This is less likely to happen if the student teacher is expected to take over the whole class right from the outset. You might have experienced this 'in at the deep end approach', but please don't put your student teachers through it. They're more likely to become confident class managers if they start with group, pair and individual work before graduating to whole-class teaching. In our partnership programme, student teachers are expected by the university to have taught at least one whole-class lesson from start to finish by the end of the first four months.

But before this big event, an effective (and a humane) way to acquaint student teachers with whole-class teaching in a 'hands-on' style is to give them a five- to ten-minute slot during a co-taught lesson. For example, you might plan a lesson with your student teacher on, let's say, Newton's Third Law of Motion (the one that explains why you go forward when you swim front crawl). In the plan, you could usefully provide an opportunity for the student teacher to teach the whole class on a particularly interesting aspect of Newton's physics: not the one about a red delicious falling on his head; how about rockets taking off? This cameo will have been rehearsed beforehand, of course, and it will give the student teacher the chance to do some real quality, short duration, didactic teaching.

Once a threshold level of competence has been achieved in these short bursts, it's time to increase the time-span to about 15–20 minutes. Longer than that isn't a good idea because the concentration of the class might start to wane. When this stage has been reached and reasonably well accomplished, it's probably helpful if you let the student go solo with some whole-class teaching up to about half an hour. At this juncture, I think it's helpful if you let the student teacher start the lesson on her or his own with a ten-minute whole-class introduction, followed by some whole-class or group activities (initiated by the student teacher, without you present).

Once these small, becoming bigger steps have been successfully accomplished, the student teacher is ready to take a whole-class lesson from start to finish on her or his own. Some interns will want you in the classroom on this occasion; others will prefer, but might be too polite to ask, to be on their own. Ask them how they want to do it, and respect their choice. If, of course, you're not in the classroom for the lesson, be on call nearby, and tell the student teacher, for assessment purposes, that it will be necessary for you to watch the next solo performance.

Co-teaching

While most secondary school teachers probably spend a lot of time teaching on their own, co-teaching is still an important skill. So don't take student teachers on a high-hill hike whose summit is solo, whole-class teaching. Provide plenty of opportunities, especially with you, for them to practise and improve their co-teaching. Now that the Department of Trade and Industry is linking all secondary schools in England and Wales to the Internet (the global computer network), co-teaching and facilitative learning look set to become increasingly important features of the new 'electronic schools'. I'm already witnessing developments of this kind in the post-16 GNVQ courses provided in my school, where teachers work in teams to support group and individualised learning. Moreover, co-teaching is a well-established feature of special needs practice, and it has long been used in all aspects of primary school teaching.

Managing misbehaviour

Opportunities for student teachers to manage the behaviour of school students are continually present in all classroom situations. But let's get down to the issue that causes perhaps most concern to student teachers in this area, namely what to do when school students misbehave. Research and our own professional experience tell us that most forms of misbehaviour are of a fairly minor nature. Thus, for example, a national teacher survey (referred to in the Elton Report, DES, 1989) noted:

> Four pupil behaviours would appear to have been common experiences for the vast majority of secondary teachers. In each case they were reported as occurring by 80 per cent or more of those in the sample. At some point during the week, then, most teachers said they had to deal with instances of pupils 'talking out of turn', 'hindering other pupils', engaging in 'calculated idleness or work avoidance' and 'not being punctual'.

Given our professional familiarity with these behaviours, we will have encountered them and routinely dealt with them in the classroom when our student teachers have been observing us. Moreover, we will have noted them too when we have observed the student teachers going through their paces. Consequently, we will have commended the effective strategies they've used in dealing with disruptive behaviour, and suggested goal-setting techniques for them to try out in future when things haven't worked out so well. Now it's time to let student teachers experiment with the tried and tested remedies, and also to give them the chance to make their own imprint.

Observing

What I'm looking for, whether as a non-participant 'fly on the wall', or as a co-teaching observer, are these qualities (emergent or actual) in intending teachers:

- An ability to get over their subject knowledge in a manner that school students of varying abilities can grasp and relate to. Good indications that this is happening/going to happen include:
  a) clarity of presentation in terms of good voice, use of clear, unambiguous language, and deployment of excellent chalkboard and/or OHP skills
  b) the pacing of learning tasks in small steps but at a fairly brisk pace
  c) the providing of on-the-spot, accurate, and where appropriate, corrective feedback
  d) most importantly, a readiness on the part of school students to perform achievable but stretching learning tasks with confidence and accuracy.
- The capacity to motivate and sustain school student learning, most readily evidenced by a high level of involvement in the task in hand and a high frequency of successful question and answer work (particularly from school student to teacher).
- That general-purpose class-management skill (or 'skills package', to be more accurate) called 'withitness'. This refers to an 'eyes in the back of the head', 'in touch with my surroundings' quality which all the best class managers exhibit in a quietly assured yet somehow 'meaning business' kind of manner.
  If you note that student teachers:
  a) arrive in the classroom before the students enter
  b) set up the learning aides they're going to use
  c) promptly carry out pre-lesson, 'first-entry' tasks (greetings, register, seating arrangements, etc.)
  d) get the lesson up and going before students have time to become flustered or distracted
  e) keep the students with them as the lesson proceeds

f) try hard to cut an engaging, purposeful presence
then they deserve full marks for 'withitness'.

When you co-teach with student teachers, your own capacity to display 'withitness' will help you get a feel of their class-management style, especially in the context of the interpersonal qualities they display. 'Is this the kind of colleague I could team-teach with?' is the question I keep in mind. Participant observation is vital if you're to get close to interactive encounters in a personal kind of way. On the other hand, it's difficult to record what's going on when you're also working alongside a colleague. Naturalness sometimes makes it hard to be objective.

Non-participant observation will, of course, make it easier to get a more focused, uninterrupted purchase on the developing class-management skills of student teachers. To begin with, I don't pre-empt my observation schedule with checklists of specific parts of a lesson (openings, closings, etc.) or discrete skills (e.g. success at initiating pair work) to watch out for. I'm more concerned, initially, with the wider canvas: Is this student teacher getting the basics right (see above, under 'withitness')? Are the class and the student teacher starting to gel? Is the student teacher making a visible effort to get organised?

After about two or three lesson observations of the non-participant type, I inform student teachers that I'll be watching for some specifics: for example, getting the right balance between didactic and interactive teaching; dealing sensitively but effectively with that persistent 'no reasonable excuse' latecomer to class; finding time to do some one-to-one tuition when the rest of the class are occupied. I think it's important that you tell student teachers – allowing for an unexpected 'barn-burning' riot on the part of the class – what the specifics are likely to be; and don't just pick out the things they had difficulties with the last time you observed them. Include some of the class-management skills that you know they're doing well at. We need some celebration of the positives, as well as the appropriate highlighting of the negatives.

I use the class-management section of my lesson observation sheet to record what, in my judgement, is either going or not going well, and I also enter constructively worded guidance – sometimes counselling student teachers to keep on as they are, but also indicating, if appropriate, target-setting strategies that might lead to improvement next time round. More about that in the next section.

Assessing

When you assess the developing classroom competences of intending teachers, the operative word to remember is 'developing'. Don't expect student teachers to perform on the level of an experienced teacher, but do look for potential. This advice might seem very obvious, but it's something I have to keep reminding myself about, especially when I start thinking 'Now why doesn't she do what I'd do in that situation?'

You've probably been around long enough in the school for school students to know your reputation. In that respect, the skills that you perform so deftly, especially in managing young people's behaviour, are largely taken for granted. By that, I mean they don't have to be as consciously planned and considered as do the 'try out' tactics of the beginning practitioner. So be an empathetic assessor.

I prefer a qualitative to a quantitative assessment style when I'm making oral and written judgements of how student teachers teach their subject and manage classes. The 'clipboard sharp' appeal of quantitative measurement doesn't always live up to its reputation, when it comes to telling a human story like it is. That said, it's not a bad idea to supplement discursive comments with a simple rating scale. Peter Tomlinson (1995), for example, uses 'open-ended report boxes' and 'tick box rating scales' in the teaching competence profile record files pioneered at Leeds University. Thus, for example, under the heading 'Interactive Teaching', which the Leeds University Secondary School Partnership interim assessment profile defines as follows:

Intelligently and effectively influences and assists pupil learning activities, organisation and resource deployment (please specify aspects and context where necessary),

mentors do the specifying in a qualitative way, as well as ticking one of six boxes: insufficient information; seriously weak; needs attention; satisfactory; strong; outstanding. In the final assessment version of this document, 'needs attention' is replaced with 'unsatisfactory'. There's also an open-ended space at the end which invites an 'action plan'.

While there's a 'quantitative fix' appeal to the tick boxes, there's also the problem, as Peter Tomlinson, to his credit, recognises, of whether the rating scale should measure the 'intended/required end-of-course level' or 'reasonable progress'. Leeds University has gone for the second of these options.

For my part, I use the lesson observation schedule illustrated in the preceding chapter (Figure 1, p. 48), which is qualitative in style. You've seen the blank format of this. Figure 2 shows the same schedule, this time completed (a fictional student teacher's name is used to protect confidentiality).

I complete this schedule during the lesson observation, and give it to the student teacher immediately afterwards. Whenever possible, I follow this up straightaway with oral feedback. This isn't always possible, however, given the

---

Assessment of DFEE Professional Competences re subject knowledge, subject application and class management

Department: *Social Sciences*   Year/Level/Subject/Topic: 12/A/*Sociology/*
                                                                                       Social Construction of Gender

Date: *20th March 95*   Time: *10.25–11.35*   Student teacher: *Joanne Griffin*

1) Subject knowledge

This is good

Up-to-date, relevant knowledge and excellent use of evidence-based data. Continuity maintained re. previous lesson by adept Q & A session on prior video viewing.
You adeptly relate subject content to students' own experiences of school-life.

Consider this advice

It's right that you linked subject knowledge to data response exam questions. However, target the content more explicitly to the syllabus.

2) Subject application

This is good

Appropriate and effective use of whole class didactic teaching and group work. Concise, punchy dictation in bite-size chunks, supported by superb chalkboard work. Clear, resonant, well-paced voice. By making the complex simple, you demonstrate effective subject application.

Consider this advice

One or two of your questions were rather leading. Consider this comment in relation to the debate on social scientific objectivity.

3) Class management

This is good

The late-arriving student looked distressed. You sensed that, and asked if she was alright rather than reprimanding her: nice touch, Joanne! Your sense of humour creates and sustains a positive learning environment.

Consider this advice

Scan the classroom a bit more vigorously. You didn't seem to notice a student who had his hand up.
Lesson closure came a little too early; get the timing right here.

Comments from student teacher (particularly goal-setting). Continue over if necessary.

Mentor/Supervising teacher:

Paul Stephens

Figure 2 A completed lesson observation schedule

practical constraints placed upon mentors. I don't know about you, but I have no designated mentoring time (I suspect this is fairly common), so I have to fit feedback sessions into my standard non-contact time. Here's an area where I think all we mentors owe it to our student teachers and to ourselves to pursue the right to have allocated mentoring time built into our already heavy timetables. How else will we be able to do our important work properly and have what we do taken seriously by senior managers and government officials?

Guiding

As mentioned in the preceding chapter, guidance needs to be provided in written form (I mainly use lesson observation schedules that contain the target-setting category 'Consider this advice'), as well as orally. The direction I provide comes under the three general headings of 'skills guidance', 'ethical guidance' and 'counselling'.

Skills guidance

While this has to relate to specific contexts, there are important teacher behaviours that are generally associated with effective teaching and class-management strategies. These are:

- Know your subject, and make sure your school students know you're an expert.
- Make learning fun, and make it exacting but achievable (it's crucial that all school students are given opportunities to succeed).
- Create and sustain a task-centred, limited focus, learning environment, in which communication between teachers and school students is maximised.
- Be quick to praise genuine effort and success, but don't make your approbation too public if you sense that this might elicit peer disapproval.
- Display school students' work (especially collaborative accomplishments) in classrooms, thereby signalling your appreciation of their achievements.
- Be in the classroom before the lesson starts. Lateness on the part of a teacher sets a bad example and is also one of the most common causes of disruptive behaviour.
- Don't leave the classroom except in an emergency. The health and safety of school students are put at risk when they're left unattended, and disruptive behaviour is much more likely. Incidentally, ensure that back-up is known to be and is available should a crisis develop in a classroom that the student teacher is unable to handle on her or his own.

Recognising that the above behaviours need to be adapted, with due sensitivity, to real classroom situations, I tell student teachers that they constitute a portfolio of practical strategies, not all of which need to be rigidly followed. It's important, though, to stress that this repertoire of 'tried and tested' professional skills should be willingly dipped into, as and when appropriate. Otherwise, everything becomes a vague, 'feel the vibes and act accordingly' meandering exercise which doesn't give student teachers the anchorage and the security that their initial forays actually need.

Ethical guidance

Above all, I tell intending teachers that theirs is a profession that makes a difference to young people's lives. Because of this, teachers can never be morally indifferent about the work they do. Teaching requires of its practitioners concern for the school student as a person, not just as a learner. Here are some helpful pointers to bear in mind when providing ethical guidance to student teachers:

- Remembering that what teachers do has important outcomes, it's crucial to maximise the public examination performances of school students. The joy of knowledge is, of course, always to be encouraged. However, when it comes to good life chances in further and higher education, and a decent, well-paid job, how well school students do in public examinations is a fundamental consideration.
- Realise that subject and pastoral concerns are integral, not distinctive. Looking after the school student as a human being shouldn't just fit into a scheduled pastoral slot.
- Show the same kind of courtesy to young people as to adults. Otherwise, it's easy to fall into the bad habit of using a 'sliding scale' model of dealing with people, whereby increasing age somehow merits more courtesy. Reflecting on this matter during the writing of this book, I recently stopped doing something that I now consider inexcusable: jumping the canteen dinner queue. When I started queuing up behind children, a 12-year-old boy said 'Thank you'.
- Involve school students in the establishment of appropriate modes of conduct. They have an impeccable sense of fair play, and when they're encouraged to deliberate in ethical affairs, it's good for them and it's just.

Counselling

Much of the counselling dispensed by mentors is designed to reduce the stress of their student teachers. Psychologists aren't entirely agreed upon what stress actually means, but a good working definition is that it constitutes a perceived gap between coping strategies and demands. Put simply, people under stress perceive that they're unable to deal with certain demands placed upon them. What seems to worry student teachers more than anything else is how to cope with disruptive classroom behaviour. While the pre-emptive and proactive strategies you've advised student teachers to use will, hopefully, keep this problem at bay for most of the time, be ready for student teachers to sometimes emerge emotionally battered from a tough lesson. On the counselling front, this is what I do:

- Make a pot of hot coffee (for both of us!) and find a comfortable place to speak with the student teacher with minimal distraction.
- Be conspicuously sympathetic and be an exceptionally good listener; make the student teacher feel free to 'tell it like it is'.
- Provide the student teacher with a reassuring and a realistic resolution. This might take a variety of forms, but when there's a real risk of repeated disruptive behaviour, consider these options: a short period of co-teaching with the intern, giving her or him the lead in the particular lesson; 'time out' from the lesson for the school student(s) causing the trouble; 'time out' for the student teacher until she or he feels ready to have another go. Make the student teacher aware that a solution to the problem is immediately available, and that things are going to work out.

Other common causes of stress (accompanied by appropriate counselling advice) include:

- The perception of not being considered a 'real' teacher by school students, especially when this is construed by the student teacher as not achieving the same standards as you. Make it clear to student teachers that if you as a mentor had to deal with 'done and dusted' interns, you'd be out of a job! As far as not getting up to my standards is concerned, I tell interns that school students often find them more stimulating than me!
- A sense of being overwhelmed by the sheer volume of tasks facing the intending teacher. Introduce student teachers to one of the best time-management specialists among your colleagues, and urge them to heed the advice they receive.
- Sudden panic triggered by feeling unable to face a particular task (typically, a tough class, next period). Don't force a student teacher to forge ahead in this situation. 'Time out', empathy and sympathy, as well as advice on a realistic strategy, are musts here.
- An awareness of institutional bullying, especially when the student teacher has the impression that she or he is treated by senior staff as something akin to a sixth former. This can be a common and a very difficult problem for

any mentor to handle, especially if the bullying is embedded in an auto-cratic, overly hierarchical management structure. Ultimately, this problem requires a whole-school solution, initiated perhaps by the professional tutor taking the matter up with those 'at the top'.

Having looked at the skill domains that are contextualised in practical class-room settings, it's now time to consider a skill that is often (but not exclusively) executed outside a roomfull of school students: assessment.

GUIDANCE POINTS _____

1 Student teachers need to test prototype lesson plans in real settings, and be ready, if necessary, to make appropriate alterations for future reference.

2 At the planning stage, mentors should provide student teachers with an accurate indication of: where particular classes are at in terms of prior knowledge and skills and ability range; what knowledge and skills are required by particular syllabuses; the kind of 'orderliness' that can realistically be expected in different classes; the prevailing norms between staff, student teachers and school students; and rules and laws pertaining to school procedures.

3 It's important that mentors liaise with other colleagues in order to let student teachers observe and work with a wide range of apposite role models.

4 Mentors should cultivate a friendly, supportive rapport with student teachers, and should treat them as professional colleagues.

5 Mentors need to be aware that differing 'subject cultures' make varying demands on class-management strategies and teaching styles.

6 Confident directiveness shouldn't be confused with 'boss management'. Even progressive teachers have to take a lead, especially when supervising school students in circumstances where health and safety issues are paramount.

7 When they demonstrate professional skills, mentors should own up if things don't always go as planned. This humility is honest and helpful to intending teachers because it shows them that making mistakes is normal.

8 It's not always necessary to signpost your demonstration lessons in advance; sometimes student teachers benefit from seeing events unfold naturally.

9 Facilitating the emerging skills of beginning teachers should usually begin through co-teaching with the mentor.

10 Mentors should pay particular attention to cultivating these skills: getting over subject knowledge; motivating; 'withitness'.

11 Observation of student teachers should include unfocused and focused methods.

12 Assessment must be objective, but remember that the student teacher isn't you: employ empathy and sympathy.

13 Qualitative assessment tells it like it is; quantitative assessment gives a purchase on calibrated progress. Use both, if possible.

14 Mentors need to provide guidance based on known effective teacher behaviours, but they also need to let student teachers find their own feet.

15 Intending teachers need to know that their future profession requires moral purpose: not least, the helping of school students to obtain a decent future.

16 School students deserve the same courtesy accorded to adults, and student teachers should be encouraged to act on this important principle.

17 Stress is a normal part of the job. That said, most of it is manageable. Moreover, what student teachers seem to fear most – disruptive behaviour – isn't as common or as severe as they imagine, and there are effective ways of dealing with it.

CHAPTER 6

Assessing school students

It's very important for mentors to emphasise that assessment which enhances a school student's sense of personal worth and success as a learner is a powerful vehicle of positive reinforcement. As the American sociologist Alex Thio (1989) notes:

> Basically, if a teacher expects certain students to fail, they are likely to do so. If a teacher expects them to succeed, then they are likely to succeed. …
> The teachers' expectations do not affect the students' performance directly, but they do influence the teachers' behaviour, which does affect students.

This assertion is supported by much research, and is commonly referred to by social scientists as a 'self-fulfilling prophecy' theory. It's a theory that should inform good classroom practice. Think about it. Teachers are rightly generous in their praise of students whom they regard as hard-working, high achievers.

When such students encounter difficulties, their teacher is likely to work extra hard to help them over the hurdle. Yet when similar problems are faced by mainstream low achievers, some (but certainly not all) teachers attribute this to lack of effort, even when the root cause might lie elsewhere.

Then there are those school students who are deemed 'smart but troublesome': the ones who know the answers but who won't toe the line. Sadly, too many of these students end up in 'low ability' sets early on in their schooling because 'rebelliousness' is seen by teachers as a disruptive influence on intellectual peers. They're thus denied access to high-level knowledge, and by the time they reach 16 many drop out of school into low-paid work and unemployment. What a waste of talent!

Teacher expectations are also sometimes linked to perceptions of 'disability', ethnicity, gender and social class. In that context, mentors must discourage intending teachers from adopting the dangerously stereotypical view that underachievement should be expected several standard deviations away from what white, middle- and upper-class male students who aren't disabled 'achieve'.

I think it's also necessary to acquaint student teachers with the current debate on teacher assessment in National Curriculum subjects. The main focus here, of course, is the extent to which we can be sure that teachers in different schools apply consistent judgements in assessing school students' performances. It would be germane, during discussions with student teachers, to point out that this issue might be successfully resolved by adopting one or a combination of these practical approaches:

- inter-school teacher moderation
- the appointment of 'national standardisers' who would act as visiting moderators
- the production of exemplifying materials
- the development of 'teacher assessor' courses, leading to professional qualifications.

Student teachers need to know that assessment doesn't take place in a vacuum. It has real contexts, and these need to be explored. It's especially important that they're encouraged to make assessments that combine humanitarian concerns with genuine objectivity. I'm thinking here of the kind of assessment that tells the truth but doesn't break the spirit, the kind that looks for progress compared to an individual's previous best rather than to the rest of the class.

While assessment of school students' achievements is conducted in many different contexts – forming a judgement during a lesson, weighing up a term's work, marking an assignment, moderating coursework with other colleagues, etc. – much, if not most, of it will be recorded in written form outside the hustle and bustle of busy classrooms. This is where, in the relative quiet of an unoc-cupied classroom, you'll do most of your mentoring on the assessment of school students' work. There will therefore be relatively little scope for classroom observation, but you'll still need to observe what student teachers have marked, as well as plan, liaise, demonstrate, facilitate, assess, and guide.

Planning

Prior to the student teachers' arrival at the school, it's a good idea to send them copies of the programmes of study and syllabuses that they're likely to be teach-ing, together with details of how these courses are assessed. If possible, give them some examples too of school students' work that you've already marked: three pieces that are reasonably representative of attainment will be fine. It will also be helpful if you give student teachers a brief, simple glossary of current assessment terminology used in schools. Here's an example of what I have in mind:

A CONCISE GUIDE TO ASSESSMENT TERMINOLOGY IN SCHOOLS

Assessment can be defined as the means by which teachers and examiners find what school students have learned, what they haven't learned, and where they're having dif-ficulties.

These are the most common forms of assessment you're likely to encounter on your school placement:

- formative assessment: the day-to-day 'measurement' of a school student's progress
- summative assessment: an end-of-key-stage or end-of-course measurement of a school student's overall performance
- criterion-referenced assessment: measuring a school student's performance against a predefined standard (the GNVQ is a good example)
- norm-referenced assessment: measuring the performance of one school student against the performances of her or his peers (most A level examinations are of this sort)
- statutory teacher assessment: a National Curriculum term that refers to teacher judgements of 'best fit' descriptions (so-called 'level descriptions') which most accurately describe a school student's overall performance.

In terms of furnishing student teachers with opportunities to find out about different types of assessment, try to construct a school placement schedule that offers them plenty of first- and second-subject marking practice, accompanied by moderating with you and other teachers. If possible, build into the schedule a seminar-style discussion between the interns, you and several colleagues (not only those who teach the interns' subjects) on how teacher assessment relates to school students' self-esteem, and on the dangers of biased measurements, especially with regard to 'disability', ethnicity, gender and social class.

Liaising

In addition to the liaison with colleagues who are prepared to be observed doing what's been described above, keep the professional tutor and the university tutors informed of how student teachers are developing as assessors. In my school, the professional tutor takes a very keen interest in feedback in this area. She's rightly concerned that the assessment of school students – particularly those taking public examinations – by student teachers is closely monitored by mentors. This ensures that the reporting back to the school students on their progress accurately reflects the assessment criteria used in relation to National Curriculum level descriptions and public examination grades.

I speak with the professional tutor about once weekly on how student teachers are faring with assessment, and I supplement this with written comments (using the university reports illustrated in Appendix 2), copied to the university and to the student teacher. While my liaison with student teachers formally takes place in our weekly meetings, I also take the opportunity to provide comments and guidance whenever I moderate their marked work. In the early stages of the school placement, quite a lot of this moderating is on a face-to-face basis. However, as student teachers become more competent assessors, I do most of the moderating when they are not actually present, returning the moderated pieces of work with written comments on a separate A4 sheet. Writing mentor comments directly onto pieces of work should be avoided. That way, school students get to read how their student teacher is doing! A separate sheet protects privacy, and gives student teachers the chance to make their own amendments before handing the marked items back to the class.

Demonstrating

Although the demonstrating of assessment isn't quite the same as a teacher showing how to make a potentially dull issue exciting and relevant, there are important opportunities for student teachers to see assessment in action. Much of this will take place outside of classrooms. Bearing that in mind, give your student teachers the chance to:

- Attend National Curriculum and public examination moderation meetings. These are as revealing of the social psychology of teacher interaction as they are of the processes – assertions, rebuttals, plea-bargaining – that lead to 'agreed-upon' final grades.
- Sit in on any meetings where whole-school assessment and recording policies are discussed, debated and formulated: for example, how records of achievement are to be set out.
- Watch teachers, individually and collaboratively, marking homework, coursework and examinations, and writing school reports, asking these colleagues for some running commentaries which explain the rationale behind their assessments. It's important that both formative and summative assessment feature here. Bearing in mind the recent growth in criterion-referenced assessment, especially in the vocational curriculum, arrange some time alongside teachers of GNVQs.
- Shadow lessons where assessments are 'live' events. These include formal assessments used, for example, in gymnastics awards and performing arts, as well as informal (usually verbal), on-task assessments that occur in all kinds of classroom situation: 'That's an outstandingly perceptive comment, Veena'; 'It doesn't look like you've revised enough for this Spanish test, Tony'.

The effective mentoring of assessment skills ultimately rests on showing student teachers how performance is measured against explicitly defined criteria before letting them have a go themselves.

Facilitating

Student teachers need plenty of opportunities to try their hand at assessment. Provided you've given them opportunities to watch experienced assessors doing the things described above, they should be ready to take the plunge. Here's what you might usefully decide to do to facilitate these initial forays, as well as to promote further development.

With written assessment:

- Select a random sample of pieces of work to be assessed (ten items or so is about right, and random selection will help to secure a representative spread), ensuring that assignments and tests are featured here.
- Get student teachers to write all their comments and calibration of scores and grades on separate sheets rather than in school students' exercise books and on assignment sheets. Do the same yourself, and then compare notes.
- When this process elicits reasonable parity between student teacher and

mentor assessment, ask the student teacher to transfer her or his comments to the real documents.

- After about three weeks or so, provided your marking and that of the student teacher are independently equivalent, it's time to give her or him responsibility for an agreed quota of written assessment, comments and marks to be written directly onto the originals. Random selection cross-marking by you – as a monitoring device – should continue right through the school placement.

With spoken assessment:

- The verbal counterpart of the first two written assessment steps should be used whenever formal assessment takes place (e.g. the grading of a solo musical recital). In practice, this means that the student teacher should confer with the mentor over the awarding of grades or scores, before this information is made public.
- Thereafter, once it's determined that the mentor and the student teacher are reaching similar conclusions, the verbal counterparts of the two other procedures used for written assessment should be used.
- In the case of more informal spoken assessments (e.g. applauding a well-turned phrase by a school student during a class discussion), less structured monitoring is usually fine. That said, it's important for the mentor to ensure, as far as is possible, that this kind of assessment is used appropriately and accurately.

Observing

Apart from watching student teachers doing the kinds of assessment task demonstrated by teachers (as described on pages 81–2), much of the observation of assessment skills will be the retroactive monitoring of marking. In practice, this means that you'll need to:

- Sit down with student teachers and, particularly in the early part of the school placement, go through all the work they've marked. Ensure, as appropriate and in measured doses, that homework, class tests, National Curriculum assignments, and public examination 'trial' papers are included.
- As confidence develops (after a few weeks would be a reasonable expectation), do as above but look at representative samples of the marked work. Of the remainder, go through about half of it without the student teacher's being present. This is mainly to assist your own time management, but it also conveys to student teachers that you don't need to over-supervise them.

- Assuming that student teachers are making progress in their assessment of school students' work, check – with or without the student teachers' being present, as appropriate – representative samples (about a third of the total).

The above procedures need to be closely integrated with your assessment of student teachers' assessment skills.

Assessing

What you'll need to assess will be, in part, subject-specific (more emphasis, for example, will be placed on recognising and rewarding creative qualities in theatre studies than in chemistry), but there are some important general features of the effective 'assessment of assessment'. These are:

- Give 'full marks' for comments that emphasise school students' achievements relative to their personal prior bests rather than to their peers.
- Check that comments and grades/scores are accurately awarded; it's very dangerous to 'skim' when you're forming a judgement about other people's ability to assess school students because sometimes the marker makes mistakes.
- Look for legible, clear comments, and for meaningful rather than bland remarks. When you and I went to school, 'fair effort' might have been a commonplace teacher comment, but it won't do today.
- Note any obvious, though not necessarily conscious, marking styles that are biased in ways that might 'short-change' the achievements of boys, girls, school students who are disabled, and working-class and ethnic minority school students.

Don't forget, when judging student teachers' ability to assess school students' work, that while your assessment must be constructive and supportive, objectivity is imperative. Niceties and politeness aside, we would be giving our school students dangerously misleading readings of their progress were we to admit imprecise assessments into the reckoning.

Moreover, objectivity in diagnostic assessment (i.e. the type that exposes areas that need improving, as well as the strengths) shouldn't be regarded as threatening because its primary goal is to measure progress. In that respect, its not an 'end-of-the-line, finished product' appraisal, but an aid to further development.

It's also important to remember that being objective in your assessment means being a good role model for the assessors of others. Being both a compassionate and an objective assessor sets an even better example.

Guiding

Skills guidance

Mentors can offer expert help here by:

- Making appropriate documentation (notably National Curriculum and public examination board assessment criteria) available to student teachers. Don't overcrowd them with too much paper at one go, though. As teachers, we all know, from the bewildering array of official documentation we receive, how unsettling this can be – especially to newcomers.
- Providing follow-up, question and answer tutorials after the student teachers have read the printed guidelines. Don't assume that student teachers will be acquainted with terms which are familiar to experienced teachers (e.g. norm-referenced assessment, level descriptions). These need full explanation.
- Offering student teachers some 'running commentary' advice while you conduct assessment which, as far as possible, relates to the prior documentation and follow-up discussion. You might, for example, talk a student teacher through your marking of an internally assessed piece of GCSE coursework. Getting other colleagues to do this too will allow interns to tap into a wider pool of professional knowledge.
- Giving student teachers the chance to put forward their own ideas. They're rightly looking to you to take the lead, but they might have some important and helpful thoughts on assessment derived from their own schooling and from mentor and tutor assessment of their performance as student teachers.

Ethical guidance

In an earlier chapter, I spoke of the need to apply 'honest compassion' when assessing the developing competences of student teachers. They, in turn, should be mindful of the same principle when they assess school students. Honesty tells the truth; compassion lifts the spirit. In that context, student teachers should be advised to:

- Generally place accurate, objective assessment before other considerations. The rigours of National Curriculum testing and public examinations require that school students receive accurate soundings of their progress. Sugar-coating what needs to be said isn't usually helpful, however kind the intention. That said, we all know of instances when, in order to keep hope alive, it's necessary to be a bit more generous than objectivity allows. This shouldn't happen too often, but student teachers might be told that a carefully selected, occasional indulgence works wonders.

- Judiciously distinguish between effort and attainment. Hard-working but relatively low-attaining school students often achieve results that change their lives: a resit C in GCSE maths that gets them onto an A level science course; two A levels at grade E that secure admission to a university. Just as intending teachers must counsel their students that 'A-grade minds combined with U-grade efforts' usually result in below-par performances, they should also praise, in the highest terms, those students who struggle intellectually but who persevere and achieve a result that makes a difference. Moreover, it's important that student teachers know that there's scope for the celebration of effort in official documents, notably records of achievement.

Counselling

School students don't take too kindly to student teachers who assess them differently from their own teachers. In my experience, this happens whether the assessment is over- or under-generous. Either way, the upshot is confusion in the mind of the school student. This is why it's vital, particularly in the early stages of their assessing, that student teachers and their mentors do a great deal of cross-marking. When, however, there's a discrepancy between intern and mentor assessment that comes to light after a piece of work has been assessed and returned, the 'correct' assessment has to take precedence over other considerations. If, in such cases, the student teacher has got it wrong, she or he needs to be told this, but simultaneously reassured that further guidance and more experience will lead to improvement.

As for the temporary 'disenchantment' that some school students might openly display to an inaccurate assessor, interns should be advised that this is a commonplace and an entirely normal – if understandably disconcerting – experience. One way of easing the surprise factor that school students encounter when they get mixed assessment messages is to tell classes beforehand to anticipate an interim 'adjustment period' when you and your student teachers get used to each other's style of marking. Hopefully, this strategy will also reduce the number of protestations that might otherwise be made before the different assessors arrive at similar conclusions.

GUIDANCE POINTS

1 School students respond better to positive than to negative teacher expectations. Get this message across to intending teachers.

2 Effective assessors tell the truth, but they don't dampen the spirit.

3   Before arriving at school, student teachers need to have access to official assessment criteria and to marked samples of school students' work.

4   There must be good liaison between mentors and other teachers concerning the accuracy of student teachers' assessment. Judging performance has important consequences, especially when school students are about to take public examinations.

5   Mentors need to provide opportunities for student teachers to observe teachers marking, doing 'live' (including spoken) assessment (e.g. performing arts auditioning), writing school reports, moderating, and, where appropriate, discussing whole-school marking policies.

6   Before 'unleashing' them on unsuspecting scripts, mentors should ensure, through moderation and the comparing of notes, that student teachers are ready for this important responsibility.

7   The retroactive monitoring of work marked by student teachers is probably the most common form of observation of assessment conducted by mentors.

8   Mentors should encourage student teachers to judge school students' work against prior personal bests, and should highlight the harmful effects of bias (e.g. failing to take account of 'gendered' performance outcomes).

9   While mentors need to emphasise that accurate assessment takes precedence over other considerations, there are rare moments when, to keep hope alive, to err on the generous side is wholly appropriate.

10 Student teachers should be told that accurate assessment requires lots of guidance and plenty of experience. They shouldn't become despondent when they get it wrong to begin with.

CHAPTER 7

Whole-school issues

It's a bit artificial to make a distinction between what goes on in classrooms and the other activities that occur in schools. Institutions are holistic, and everything that happens in them – how school students behave in corridors, whether teachers bark 'You there, come here', or show some civility when they address young people – makes a contribution to the overall ethos. That said, it's conventional these days to define whole-school mentoring (sometimes referred to as 'phase mentoring'; I've no idea why!) as those aspects of school-based initial teacher education that aren't subject-specific. It doesn't matter whether your student teachers are going to teach maths, law, English, psychology, or tourism and leisure, their professional brief must encompass important whole-school issues like these:

- tuning into school and community cultures, and adopting appropriate behaviours, while maintaining private moralities
- developing effective pastoral skills, and infusing these skills with a genuinely caring spirit

- becoming good administrators, especially in the area of computer applications
- cultivating excellent human relations skills when liaising with colleagues and parents
- informing good practice with the insights of social scientific research.

No doubt one could add to the above list, but these areas are distilled from the main whole-school issues contained in the DfE Circular 9/92 'professional development' competence. Some of the criteria included in this umbrella competence overlap with other broad competences. For example, teacher expectations (a 'professional development' competence) necessarily links with the 'assessment' competence, and has consequently been addressed in the preceding chapter. In such instances, this chapter will not deal again with issues already covered.

Planning

By sending student teachers appropriate documentation (notably a school prospectus and departmental guidelines) prior to their arrival at school, you can give them a taste of things to come. It's very important that they become quickly familiarised with the 'official' norms and values of the school and of the culture of the surrounding community.

Here are some extracts from a preamble that I send to student teachers of different subjects before they start their first placement with us:

Welcome to the school. It's a large comprehensive school (1800 students) on the outskirts of a nearby city. The school is located in a predominantly white working-class neighbourhood.
In terms of its official ethos, the school is tough on discipline, and it encourages a high level of conforming behaviour.

This thumbnail sketch says quite a lot to the discerning reader. But it needs to be made more explicit when the student teachers arrive on site. In that context, you could helpfully build these 'culture cue' experiences into your whole-school issues programme:

- A walking tour of the school's neighbourhood, hosted by mentors and, if possible, some local parents. Lots of cues can be picked up here: is the area multi-ethnic? Is extensive poverty evident? Is the 'other side of the tracks' phenomenon apparent (very obviously prosperous, mainly private residential areas backing onto run-down council estates)? Are there churches, mosques and synagogues around?

- A tour of the school, hosted by school students. Student teachers should be encouraged to talk quite openly with their guides (who, in turn, should be advised not to comment on individual teachers and other staff by name). They should also get a feel of the sometimes understated cultural agenda of the school, as revealed, for example, by the presence or absence of wall displays that celebrate the achievements of women in science, of black history, of human rights activists.

As far as the planning of pastoral encounters is concerned, try to give student teachers the chance to meet and talk with form tutors, heads of year, a deputy headteacher and the headteacher. These colleagues are usually adept administrators too, so encourage student teachers to tap into their expertise. This will, of course, require forward planning, so get your school diary out early in order to book your colleagues' valuable time.

Ensure too that the observation of collective worship, if it occurs in the school, and, whenever possible, of the teaching of religious education, and personal, health and social education, is provided for in the whole-school issues plan. The law, as stated in the Education Reform Act (1988), requires schools to attend to the moral and spiritual well-being of school students, and this requirement is firmly anchored within DfE Circular 9/92.

Although teachers of religious education and personal, health and social education might be more explicitly involved in the moral and spiritual aspects of teaching than teachers of other subjects, all teachers have to address these matters, whatever their personal beliefs. So be mindful, when you draw up a whole-school issues schedule, of the need to give student teachers occasion to observe, and, as relevant, to participate in those areas of school life.

In order to remind student teachers that effective practice can be enhanced by the findings of social scientific research, it's helpful to insert a one-day workshop on recent school improvement strategies into the whole-school issues programme. More than anything else, this is an area where mentors can impress upon intending teachers the need for grounded theory (that is, theory which is evidence-based) to inform effective practice. Why not invite some university tutors to this event?

Liaising

In addition to the liaison needed to implement the planned activities described in the preceding section, I think it gives student teachers a 'whole-school' feel of things if you introduce them to as many of these important colleagues as possible: caretakers, office staff, canteen staff and cleaners. Effective schools adopt collegiate, holistic outlooks, where 'hierarchy' is less important than team spirit, where everyone's opinion and dignity counts. These aren't heady platitudes: they're felt convictions. Where I work, when staff forums are held to discuss and influence school policy, every employee has the right to be there, the right to be heard, and the right to cast a vote. And they exercise those rights. Teachers and other colleagues, as well as school students, parents and governors also marched together recently in protest over environmental degradation caused by the opening of an open-cast coal mine. That's what I call 'esprit de corps'!

The liaison between mentors and student teachers on whole-school issues doesn't always involve assessment. In this area, I only assess the student teachers who teach my subject, generally using official reports and oral feedback. When it comes to other student teachers, I'm more a provider of information than a judge of performance. That said, when one of them does something 'above and beyond the call of duty', like voluntarily helping out on recess duty, I readily send a letter to the university commending this readiness to 'get stuck in'.

Demonstrating

Because whole-school issues don't always follow a preplanned schedule (like how I recently had to break up a fight between two boys during the dinner hour, one of whom didn't even attend the school!), shadowing is probably the best form of demonstration a mentor can provide. This should involve at least one day from start to finish shadowing you – and try to pick a day when you antic-ipate plenty of variety in the tasks you perform. If possible, arrange for your stu-dent teachers to shadow at least one other colleague – not necessarily a teacher – for up to half a day.

Shadowing should, whenever possible, extend to:

- Parents' evenings. I also invite some participation here if the student teach-ers want to offer appropriate comments. Many student teachers only get to meet parents after they qualify. This shouldn't be the case.
- Staff and departmental meetings. Again, as appropriate, student teachers are welcome to make contributions during my departmental meetings.
- School journeys and educational visits. My social sciences student teachers attended an annual A level conference recently, not just to observe myself and other teachers, but also to lead a workshop on women's studies.

As said earlier, the generic skills that form the basis of good mentoring do over-lap. So don't be concerned if, as above, a bit of watching – even the non-partic-ipant kind – turns into a bit of doing.

Facilitating

There's so much going on in the realm of whole-school issues that it's sometimes best to focus on a few specific areas where student teachers need to get involved. Here are some examples of 'specifics' that I think are especially important:

- Arrange for student teachers to work alongside teachers of children with special needs. Working with these colleagues provides a wonderful 'apprenticeship' in understanding how to enhance the learning potential and the self-esteem of school students whom some people erroneously regard as 'failures'.
- Have student teachers assist form tutors. Co-working should lead eventually to letting student teachers take over for some of the time.
- Provide opportunities for student teachers to gain practice in the management of students outside of classrooms. Managing young people as they move about the school, let off steam in the playground, line up for dinner, and do other things which require supervision, is just as important as their management within the classroom.

Obviously, you might decide to add to this list. Suffice it to say that it's better for student teachers to do a few things well rather than skim lots of tasks superficially.

Observing

The observation of student teachers' involvement in whole-school issues isn't usually of the 'clipboard recording' style. It's better – and fairer on them – to get a feel of their readiness to go beyond classroom teaching. In my school, recess corridor supervision and bus-bay duties figure prominently here. How better to judge my student teachers' 'crowd control' skills than to watch them in these, the ultimate 'battlegrounds'?

My preference is decidedly for participant observation. But, whenever possible, I try to give student teachers the lead, and I don't make my presence too conspicuous. For example, I had a student teacher patrolling a potentially rowdy part of a corridor recently during a recess, while I kept in a fairly central part of the area. That way, I could see what the student teacher was doing, but school students didn't have the impression that I was over-supervising her. Had they sensed that, some of them might have given her a hard time on the assumption that she needed my back-up.

Beyond the more visible aspects of whole-school issues, eyeball observation isn't really an option. How, for example, can a mentor 'observe' an intern reading up on teachers and the law, or researching how social background affects achievement? So how do we mentors go about gauging progress on the whole-school issues front? This point is addressed in the next section.

Assessing

Getting a feel of the extent to which student teachers successfully become a part of the broader canvas during their school-based programme can't be done on a rating scale: 'Toby scores 7/10 for volunteering to do a canteen duty, but only 3/10 because he couldn't stop the children from cheering when one of the boys dropped a plate'. It doesn't work, does it?

Better to develop a sense of what these student teachers are doing beyond the usual 'routine' of class teaching. Are they beginning to conduct themselves like teachers: handling form administration confidently, circulating in the staffroom, attending after-school events, and generally identifying with the wider frame? It's this readiness to behave on a holistic rather than a particular-istic level that's the hallmark of good work in a whole-school issues sense. In that respect, what we're looking for is something akin to a Renaissance quality: an all-rounded as opposed to a narrow outlook.

Aside from giving student teachers oral feedback on the impressions I have about their 'all-roundedness', I also put my written observations in the univer-sity's pro-forma reports, under the category of 'professional development'. Qualitative assessment is the preferred mode here, and typical comments are exemplified in Appendix 2.

Guiding

Skills guidance

Among the most important skills guidance you can offer student teachers in the area of whole-school issues is how to be discerning and effective applicants for first teaching appointments. This begins with establishing what their expertise and qualifications are, what experiences they will have acquired by the end of initial teacher education, and seeing if all this is likely to get them short-listed for the kind of post they're after. Being realistic but not unadventurous is what's needed. Then it's time to scour the local education authority vacancy lists and the newspapers that advertise national vacancies (notably the *Times Educational Supplement* and the Tuesday edition of the *Guardian*).

In most instances, student teachers will be expected to request a job description and an application form for any position that they're interested in. When these arrive, you'll be a much-appreciated mentor if you offer to go through the job description (look out for any tell-tale signs that might reveal important information) with the potential applicant, as well as providing expert guidance on how to fill in an application form, prepare a curriculum vitae, and write a covering letter. I also offer student teachers 'dry-run' interviews.

Most schools short-list up to about five or so applicants for a first appointment interview. Then, pending satisfactory references (I always offer to be a referee), they usually adopt the rather brutal practice of appointing the successful candidate and dismissing the unsuccessful candidates immediately after the interview. Tell your student teachers that they'll normally be expected to accept or reject a job offer on the spot. On the other hand, if they're not offered the post, they should be encouraged to ask for a diagnostic debriefing.

In terms of other important whole-school issues, I offer my student teachers this skills guidance:

- Get used to keeping a professional diary; time management won't be possible without one.
- Learn some basic IT skills, especially how to word process and how to use data bases and spreadsheets.
- Acquire three plastic wallet files and three corresponding trays, each pair designated *Form*, *Subject* and *Other*; they'll fill up quickly!
- Consider taking a course in public speaking; not only will this assist intending teachers to cut an impressive presence in class and during assemblies, it will help them to keep laryngitis and other throat ailments at bay. York University actually provides its student teachers with a session on 'voice care'.

Ethical guidance

The section on planning referred to the principle that schools are expected to be involved in the transmission of moral and spiritual values. Whether your student teachers are Bhuddists, Christians, Hindus, Jews, Moslems, followers of other faiths, atheists or agnostics, they'll be expected to foster, through their habits and teaching, certain principles. It's not for me to be prescriptive here, but I suggest that intending teachers should be made mindful of the need to:

- Encourage school students to be tolerant, and to recognise that people express their cultural and spiritual nature in many different ways. At the same time, it's important that unjust practices (e.g. racism) should never be tolerated, even if such actions masquerade under the pretext of 'individual freedoms'.
- Deal with matters concerning sexual and other sensitive areas of personal

behaviour in an objective rather than a judgemental manner. I don't think that school students take too kindly to being 'preached at', but I sense that they're ready to listen to evidence.

- Be alert to any signs of child abuse – physically injurious, sexual, emotional and neglect – and be aware of school procedures in this area. It's vital that intending teachers know who to turn to in matters of suspected child abuse. They should also be acquainted with the correct forms of confidentiality in order to minimise the risk of stigmatisation to children and families.

Counselling

Stress that's induced by disruptive behaviour on the part of school students is sometimes more commonly linked to teacher supervision in corridors and canteens than with what goes on in classrooms. When school students have a measure of social space outside the more structured environment of the classroom, they can sometimes be more boisterous in their behaviour.

Teachers need to recognise this as something fairly natural, and I think it's important that mentors advise student teachers to allow for and accept it, instead of trying to fight a battle they can't and don't need to win. Can you imagine telling some twenty or so Year 11 students who are behaving somewhat loudly in a corridor during a recess that they must remain silent until the bell goes? It's an unrealistic and, dare I say, an unreasonable expectation. The loud, boisterous behaviour among teachers in my school staffroom needs to be heard to be believed! Who doesn't have the right to let off steam after a tough classroom session, whether it's a school student or a teacher?

Another potent source of stress in the whole-school issues domain is the demand made upon teachers by school students – and sometimes parents – as 'social workers' and confidants. Student teachers should be encouraged to show compassion, understanding and tact if they encounter school students whose parents are so poor that they can't afford to buy a gym shirt for a son or daughter, or if a child confides that she or he is being bullied. I don't accept the view that teachers should pass all such problems on to senior management or outside agencies. However, student teachers should be advised that these 'lifelines' exist, if they need or want to use them. There's nothing so daunting as the thought that one alone has to take full responsibility for what seems like an intractable problem in the life of a school student.

Schools are bigger than individual teachers, and good schools have an *esprit de corps*, a common vision, a community spirit, characterised by a willingness to share and solve problems together. That's why, at the heart of effective counselling and of effective mentoring in general, there's a readiness by mentors to be each sister's, each brother's, keeper.

GUIDANCE POINTS _____

1   Mentors need to impress upon student teachers that schools are holistic, and have their own cultures and styles.

2   A pre-placement tour of the school and its neighbourhood gives student teachers invaluable insights.

3   Encourage student teachers to spend time with and talk to caretakers, canteen staff, cleaners, office staff, parents and governors, as well as teachers.

4   If possible, arrange a one-day workshop on whole-school issues that are informed by recent and relevant research (e.g. school improvement strategies)

5   Shadowing is arguably the best way to let student teachers 'observe' whole-school issues.

6   It's better for student teachers to try their hand at a few important whole-school tasks than to take on too much and spread their experiences thinly.

7   When you observe and assess the performance of student teachers in the area of whole-school issues, participant observation and qualitative assessment are especially suitable.

8   Help student teachers secure a first appointment. They'll appreciate advice on how to write applications and CVs, and will gain much from 'dry-run' interviews.

9   Stress is common, but it can usually be tackled with tried and tested measures, and by making student teachers aware that they're part of a team.

Afterword

Mentors have access to 'intelligent practical knowledge' that is derived from reflection and experience. In that respect, they have what John Furlong (1995b) describes as 'knowledge that is ... essentially practical but which nevertheless involves an implicit appreciation of the complexities on which it is based'.

Effective mentoring takes teacher education beyond an apprenticeship. For newly qualified teachers require much more than 'tricks of the trade' guidance. Learning to teach is about learning how to practise professional skills with good judgement. 'Recipe knowledge' sometimes provides helpful generic pointers, but teachers also need to relate their practice to changing circumstances. This is why mentors need to strike the right balance between offering certain generalisable insights, and giving student teachers the confidence to cue into particular contexts.

At the beginning of their teacher education programme, student teachers understandably expect their mentors to supply some 'basic survival' strategies. In that context, how to start a lesson, how to take a register, and how to deal with 'common or garden variety' misbehaviours are especially important. Tried and tested tactics have their place, and they offer coherence and security to both teachers and school students. But as the course proceeds, student teachers must be given opportunities to experiment, to try out the advice that has been dispensed, to begin to cultivate their own personal style, and to reflect upon the outcomes. In short, they must be allowed some original thoughts.

They should also be encouraged to get to grips with fundamental ethical and intellectual issues, like the teacher's role in promoting social justice, and the implications of educational research for professional practice. Such matters aren't simply confined to campus-based discussion with academic tutors. They're an integral part of conscientious, informed and principled practice. It's for the mentor to show student teachers how teaching is both a cognitive and a moral venture, and a form of professional work that needs to be refined and improved through experience and continuous study.

Your job, as a mentor, is to help student teachers to become competent and reflective practitioners who, when they achieve Qualified Teacher Status, are prepared and ready to enter a profession that makes a difference. You have important work ahead.

APPENDIX 1

The National Curriculum (England and Wales) made easy: A concise guide for student teachers

The National Curriculum applies to students of compulsory school age in maintained schools. It is introduced through four **key stages**. In broad terms, these are:

	Students' ages	Year groups
Key Stage 1	5–7	1–2
Key Stage 2	7–11	3–6
Key Stage 3	11–14	7–9
Key Stage 4	14–16	10–11

In England, the National Curriculum subjects for the key stages indicated are:

Key Stages 1 and 2   English, mathematics, science, technology (design and technology, and information technology), history, geography, art, music, and physical education

Key Stage 3   As at Key Stages 1 and 2, plus a modern foreign language

Key Stage 4   English, mathematics, science, and physical education; and, from August 1996, technology (design and technology, and information technology), and a modern foreign language.

In Wales, the National Curriculum subjects for the key stages indicated are:

Key Stages 1 and 2   English (except at Key Stage 1 in Welsh-speaking classes), Welsh, mathematics, science, technology (design and technology, and information technology), history, geography, art, music, and physical education

Key Stage 3   As at Key Stages 1 and 2, plus a modern foreign language

Key Stage 4   English, Welsh (except in non-Welsh-speaking schools until 1999) mathematics, science, and physical education.

Programmes of Study describe what students should be taught in each subject and for each key stage.

Attainment Targets define the standards of performance expected of students.

At the end of Key Stages 1, 2, and 3, standards of performance expected of students in all subjects except art, music, and physical education are set out in **level descriptions**. There are eight level descriptions, and an additional description above Level 8 for exceptional performance.

End of key stage descriptions set out the standards of performance expected of the majority of students at the end of each key stage in art, music and physical education. Descriptions of exceptional performance may be used in art and music at the end of Key Stage 3, and in physical education at the end of Key Stage 4.

Public examinations are the principal means of assessing performance at Key Stage 4. New GCSE syllabuses that incorporate the revised National Curriculum will be introduced for courses beginning in September 1996.

Special educational needs

The revised National Curriculum gives teachers a lot more flexibility to respond to the requirements of school students who have special needs. In particular, teachers are provided with more scope to give these students appropriately challenging work at each key stage. This should help to reduce instances of National Curriculum modifications and disapplications for school students, either temporarily at the headteacher's discretion, or through a statement of special educational needs.

APPENDIX 2

Mentor reports

Settling-in Report on PGCE student attached to Department of Social Sciences for Spring Term 1994

For the attention of:
Dr Ian Davies
Department of Educational Studies
University of York
Heslington Lane
YORK
YO1 5DD

12 January 1994

Student   Philip Costello
Main teaching subject and level   Sociology (A Level)
Other teaching subject(s) and level(s)   Psychology (A Level)
Personal and Social Education (KS4)

1 **General remarks and classroom observations**
Philip has adopted a positive attitude to all aspects of initial teacher education, and he is eager to receive objective feedback.
In the classroom, Philip strives to make complex issues simple, to make his subject interesting, and to link it to the personal experiences of his students. He succeeds on all counts.

2 **Student feedback**
Philip's students like him and they appreciate his meticulously prepared handouts. Moreover, they appreciate his sense of humour, kind disposition and his concern for both their academic development and their general well-being.

3 **Staff feedback**
Social Sciences colleagues and other staff note that Philip is thoroughly competent, very reliable, and that he is easy to work with.

4 **Concluding remarks**
Philip's sheer energy and commitment both in and outside the classroom make me confident that he will eventually achieve a position of substantial seniority when he enters the teaching profession.

5 Agreed goals

These goals have been identified by Philip and have received the concurrence of his subject mentor, Paul Stephens.

(i)   continuing to mix and match individual, group and whole-class teaching.
(ii) continuing to pitch tasks at appropriate cognitive levels.
(iii) to gain substantial experience in the recording and assessment of students' work.

Mentor's name and signature: **Dr Paul Stephens (Head of Social Sciences)**

Paul Stephens

Philip Costello

Student's signature   -----------------------------------

University of York
Department of Educational Studies

Half-term Statement February 1995

Student: Joanne Griffin School: North England Comprehensive

In the light of discussions on your progress, it has been agreed that:

✔ a) So far, **your progress has been satisfactory** and we fully expect you to complete this school placement successfully.

b) So far, **your progress indicates a need for improvement** in the areas indicated below. While you must work at these areas yourself, your tutor/s will offer additional support. If there is insufficient evidence of improvement, then you may need to be visited by an external examiner.

c) So far, **your progress causes us to be concerned** that you may not be able to demonstrate a satisfactory level of competence by the end of term. Our particular concerns are detailed below. While you must work at these areas yourself, your tutor/s will offer additional support. It is highly likely that you will be visited by an external examiner.

Our concerns are:

Signed on behalf of the school: *Paul Stephens*

I have read the above statement on my progress

Student's signature: *Joanne Griffin*

This form to be returned completed before the half-term break to the University of York Department of Educational Studies (s.a.e. enclosed).

103

University of York
Department of Educational Studies

PGCE Spring Term Progress Review (General orientation)

Student: Joanne Griffin   Tutor: Paul Stephens (Mentor)

School: North England Comprehensive   Visit date: N/A
(refers to Jan/Feb 95)
Visit no.: N/A

Comments are made where appropriate in relation to the statements of competence, and provide a general progress report as well as specific comments on particular lessons.

Subject knowledge
Excellent. Joanne's use of relevant, up-to-date resources has been much appreciated by her sociology students. A familiarity with the latest research is precisely what they need in order to do well in the A Level.

Subject application
By mixing complex issues understandable to all students, and by making her subject knowledge stimulating and relevant to students' real lives and felt convictions, Joanne has excelled on this front.

Class management
A very confident presence, coupled with a kind, generous disposition, has kept disruptive behaviour at bay. Joanne is impeccably fair-minded, and this quality is very well received by her students. Their high rate of on-task engagement demonstrates Joanne's ability to motivate. Her lessons are full of variety and make full and effective use of whole-class and group teaching techniques.

Assessment and recording
Very precise assessment, accurately recorded. Joanne is honest about students' progress, but highly supportive when there is scope for improvement.

Professional development
An exceptionally talented, very professional colleague who is never averse to getting 'stuck into' whole-school issues. Joanne's contributions to a forthcoming social sciences conference are particularly welcomed. She is a very adept communicator, and is very popular indeed with both students and staff.

Paul Stephens   1 March 1995

Dr Paul Stephens   Head of Social Sciences/ITE Mentor

University of York
Department of Educational Studies

PGCE Spring Term Progress Review (Lesson observation)

Student: Veena Sembhy   Tutor: Paul Stephens (Mentor)

School: North England Comprehensive   Visit date: 1 February 1995
                                          Visit no.:   4th

Comments are made where appropriate in relation to the statements of competence, and provide a general progress report as well as specific comments on particular lessons.

This review principally refers to the observation, over thirty minutes, of part of an A Level Sociology lesson with a class of Lower Sixth students who are generally keen and committed. The topic was 'theories of education'.

Subject knowledge, as is always the case, was supported by sound research, and, today, by relevant references to preceding video viewings of documentaries on Eton and Summerhill. The lesson plan was very well organised and realistic.

Subject application is excellent: Veena has a good voice, and she is one of the best exponents of chalkboard work I have come across. It is also very evident that she is succeeding in making complex theoretical issues clear and vivid by relating them to real-life events. Questions were testing but not beyond what the students could reasonably manage: the right balance has been struck here.

Class management was confident and supportive. It is right that Veena moves around the classroom, eliciting individual responses from students and making them all feel that they have something to contribute. On-task praise is given in the right doses, which encourages this already animated class to know that they are making real progress.

While *assessment and recording* rightly did not feature in this lesson, Veena is an accurate and sympathetic assessor and recorder. She is 'bang on target' as far as examining board marking criteria are concerned, and her encouraging comments make even the lower achieving students feel that they are capable of improving.

As far as *professional development* is concerned, Veena conducts herself like a qualified practitioner. She goes well beyond the normal brief, by attending departmental and off-site meetings, by assuredly doing recess and end of school duties, and by broadening her portfolio by teaching and observing National Curriculum Geography and Year 10 and 11 Personal and Social Education. Staff and students are impressed by your unstinting professionalism, Veena. So am I.

Paul Stephens   *1 February 1995*
Dr Paul Stephens   Head of Social Sciences/ITE Mentor

FINAL MENTOR REPORT: VEENA SEMBHY

Subject knowledge
Excellent knowledge of sociology, good second subject knowledge of geography, thoroughly competent work in personal, health and social education and GNVQ Advanced Business & Finance. Outstanding reports from social sciences, geography, PHSE and GNVQ colleagues. Veena makes complex issues accessible to all her students: what more could one ask for from an effective teacher?

Subject application
Invigorating and captivating presentations that employ a wide range of apposite resources, including IT and audiovisual learning aids. Great voice and possibly the best chalkboard work I have ever come across. Veena gets maximum potential from her students by motivating them.

Class management
Assured, poised, fair-minded, approachable, kind, in control without being heavy-handed; no disruptive behaviour on the part of any students (lower school included) observed. Their sustained on-task application shows Veena's skills in maintaining positive behavioural and effective learning outcomes. She adeptly deploys whole-class and group teaching techniques, and I have received outstanding feedback on her pastoral work from the form teacher.

Assessment and recording
Very precise, but also takes into consideration the need of students to feel encouraged and supported. Veena's spoken and written reporting of students' progress is consistently exemplary.

Professional development
One of my best ever student teachers: reliable; engaged in whole-school as well as subject issues; voluntarily attends parents' evenings, Association of Teachers of Social Sciences meetings at Leeds Metropolitan University etc. Is also contributing significantly to a national social sciences conference for A Level students at the same university. Veena's rapport with all colleagues and students is superb. We're sorry indeed to see her go.

Paul Stephens
Dr Paul Stephens   Head of Social Sciences/ITE Mentor
23 March 1995

APPENDIX 3

Pro-forma lesson plan

THE UNIVERSITY OF YORK
DEPARTMENT OF EDUCATIONAL STUDIES

History/Sociology PGCE   *Lesson Plan Format*   Veena Sembhy
                                                       – Lesson 9

Class L6B	Period 7/8	Date 1st Feb 95

Aim (to include relevant National Curriculum information)
To introduce a critique of Meritocracy using the example of public schools. Show how the structure of schools differs according to who they are catering for – i.e. different messages are being introduced. Following Part(b) of the education section of the syllabus.

Resources *Blackboard*

Timings	Teacher Action	Pupil Action
5 mins.	Register	Settle down
5 mins.	Ask questions about Summerhill video → Discussion	Answering questions and discussing Summerhill video.
10 mins.		Answer questions relating to Summerhill + structures of schools.
5 mins.	Conclusion i.e. what Marxists + Functionalists would say about Summerhill.	Listen + make notes.
5 mins.	Introduce the rest of the lesson – Public schools – why a critique of Meritocracy.	Listen.
5 mins.		What is Meritocracy? Discuss verbally – i.e. Marxist + Functionalist views.
10 mins.	Lead discussion on Eton video.	Participate in discussion on Eton. Get into groups of 2.
5 mins.		BRAINSTORM: which are the major public schools?
5 mins.	Give some stats about public schools	Write info. down.
10 mins.		Answer questions based on discussions earlier (write down).
5 mins.	Explain Reading + Homework BILTON P312–318	(Summarise 313 from 2nd paragraph)

Evaluation The lesson worked well. They were all keen to comment on the video and became engaged in some relevant discussions. By getting them into groups everyone had something to say. But they had so much to say about the video that the end of the lesson became a bit rushed – I should have watched the time more carefully.

Bibliography

Black, Desiree and Booth, Martin (1992) 'Commitment to Mentoring', pp. 29–42. In Wilkin, Margaret (ed.) *Mentoring in Schools*. London: Kogan Page.

Bridges, David (1995) 'School-Based Teacher Education', pp. 64–80. In Kerry, Trevor and Shelton Mayes, Ann (eds) *Issues in Mentoring*. London: Routledge.

Brown, Sally and McIntyre, Donald (1993) *Making Sense of Teaching*. Milton Keynes: Open University Press.

Calderhead, James (1992) 'Can the Competences of Teaching be Accounted for in Terms of Competences? Contrasting Views of Professional Practice from Research and Policy'. Discussion Paper presented at UCET Annual Conference, Oxford.

Carr, David (September 1993) 'Questions of Competence', pp. 253–71. *British Journal of Educational Studies*, Vol. 41, No. 3.

Davies, Ian, and Macaro, Ernesto (Summer 1995) 'The Reactions of Teachers, Tutors and Students to Profiling Student Competences in Initial Teacher Education' pp. 28–41. *Journal of Further and Higher Education*, Vol. 19, No. 2.

Department for Education (DfE) (1992) *Initial Teacher Training (Secondary Phase)*. *Circular No 9/92*. London: DfE.

Department for Education (DfE) (1993a) *The Government's Proposals for the Reform of Initial Teacher Training*. London.

Department for Education (DfE) (1993b) *The Initial Training of Primary School Teachers: New Criteria for Courses*. *Circular No 14/93*. London.

Department of Education and Science (DES) (1989) *Discipline in Schools* (The Elton Report). London: HMSO.

Edwards, Tony (1994) 'The Universities Council for the Education of Teachers: Defending an Interest or Fighting a Cause?', pp. 143–52. *Journal of Education for Teaching*, Vol. 20, No. 2.

Furlong, John (1995a) 'The Limits of Competence: A Cautionary note on Circular 9/92', pp. 225–31. In Kerry, Trevor, and Shelton Mayes, Ann (eds) *Issues in Mentoring*. London: Routledge.

Furlong, John (1995b) 'Higher Education and Initial Teacher Training: A Changing Relation', pp. 35–48. In Kerr, David, and O'Neill, Cliff (eds) *Professional Preparation and Professional Development in a Climate of Change.* Standing Conference of History Teacher Educators in the United Kingdom, in association with the University College of St Martin, Lancaster.

Furlong, John and Maynard, Trisha (1995) *Mentoring Student Teachers.* London: Routledge.
This book strikes the right balance between academic discourse and practical relevance. It usefully documents the authors' research into the nature of school-based, professional learning, and what this means for the work of the mentor.

Hagger, Hazel, Burn, Katharine and McIntyre, Donald (1993) *The School Mentor Handbook.* London: Kogan Page.
Available in ring-binder format (for ease of photocopying), and, from 1995, in paperback, this is a good, practical guide to secondary school mentoring. The Handbook is based on the Oxford Internship Scheme, but is a reference book rather than a training manual. While it has little to say about whole-school issues, it helpfully draws upon the classroom expertise of Oxford mentors in a way that makes the task of mentoring easier for others.

Haigh, Gerald (1995) *Times Educational Supplement,* 10 February.

Kerry, Trevor and Shelton Mayes, Ann (eds) (1995) *Issues in Mentoring.* London: Routledge.
This reader is an excellent guide to 'intelligent practice' for mentors and education tutors. It examines mentoring in a wide variety of settings, from primary school to college.

Kozol, Jonathan (1993) *On Being a Teacher.* Oxford: Oneworld Publications.

McIntyre, Donald (1990) 'Ideas and Principles Guiding the Internship Scheme', pp. 17–33. In Benton, Peter (ed.) *The Oxford Internship Scheme.* London: Calouste Gulbenkian Foundation.

Murray, Frank (1995) *Times Educational Supplement,* 10 February.

Report of the Commission on Global Governance (1995) *Our Global Neighbourhood.* Oxford: Oxford University Press.

Rothwell, S., Nardi, E., and McIntyre, D. (1994) 'The Perceived Values of the Role Activities of Mentors and Curricular, Professional and General Tutors', pp. 19–39. In Reid, Ivan, Constable, Hilary and Griffiths, Roy (eds) *Teacher Education Reform.* London: Paul Chapman.

Sammons, Pam, Hillman, Josh and Mortimore, Peter (1995) *Times Educational Supplement,* 17 March.

Stephens, Paul (1995) 'Principled Mentoring and Competency-Driven Teacher Education in an Urban Comprehensive School', pp. 100–11. In Griffiths, Vivienne and Owen, Patricia (eds) *Schools in Partnership*. London: Paul Chapman.

Stones, Ed (1993), cited by Scrimger, Sue, in 'A Critique of the Work of Professor E. Stones', pp. 157–62. In Gilroy, Peter and Smith, Michael (eds) *International Analyses of Teacher Education*. Carfax Publishing Company, no publication location given.

Teacher Training Agency (1994) *Profiles of Teacher Competences: Consultation on Draft Guidance*. London.

Thio, Alex (1989) *Sociology: An Introduction* (2nd edition). New York: Harper & Row.

Tomlinson, Peter (1995) *Understanding Mentoring*. Milton Keynes: Open University Press.
This book arose out of Peter Tomlinson's work as an education tutor in the Leeds University Secondary School Partnership PGCE Scheme. It offers practical strategies for school mentors which are mainly based on psychological research into 'intelligent skill' development. The book is written in a fairly academic style, and is an excellent resource for mentors who are studying for higher degrees in the area of teacher education.

Whyte, William Foote (1943) *Street Corner Society* (3rd edition 1981). Chicago: University of Chicago Press.

Willis, Paul (1988) *Learning to Labour: How Working Class Kids Get Working Class Jobs*. Aldershot: Gower.

Wragg, E. C. (1993) *Primary Teaching Skills*. London: Routledge.

Index